REASONS FOR HOPE

CHRIST COMMUNITY CHURCH
BEAVERTON, OREGON

GOOD CATCH PUBLISHING

Copyright © 2005 by Christ Community Church, Beaverton, Oregon

All rights reserved. Written permission must be secured from the publisher to use or reproduce any part of this book, except for brief quotations in critical reviews or articles.

Published in Beaverton, Oregon, by Good Catch Publishing.
www.goodcatchpublishing.com

Printed in the United States of America

Contents

	Introduction	13
Chapter 1	Hope After the Death of a Child	17
Chapter 2	Hope After Child Abuse	33
Chapter 3	Hope For a New Identity	65
Chapter 4	Hope For an Alcoholic	89
Chapter 5	Hope for Overcoming Compulsive Anger	109
Chapter 6	Hope for an Abused Wife	119
Chapter 7	Hope For Chronic Pain	137
Chapter 8	Hope For a Struggling Family	155
Chapter 9	Hope After Despair	185
	Conclusion	205

Introduction

"Were it not for hope the heart would break."
—**Scottish Proverb**

What do you do when your dreams have just gone up in smoke, when you have lost everything and there is no place to turn, when your last shred of hope is gone? Maybe you have been there and felt the empty despair. Or maybe you are there right now, and you are saying, "Why go on? My life is hopeless. There is nothing I can do!"

This little book you hold in your hands contains the simple stories of people who felt like that. But what looked like a dead end to them was only a jog in the road, which turned into a breakthrough. The hope they found led them to a new life—a better, richer life than they had ever known.

As you read these stories, resist the thought that says, "Good story, but that could never happen to me." Remember, these are real people who turned a corner and discovered a whole new life. Keep reminding yourself: ***Reasons for Hope Are Closer Than They Appear!*** You are just moments from a discovery that can bring you the life you always dreamed of!

1

HOPE AFTER THE DEATH OF A CHILD

SHARON

We waited at the locked door while phoning the desk for permission to enter. Our identity was established and we were cleared. The solid click of the lock release echoed through the waiting area. First was the long, hushed hallway and then a little alcove with four stainless steel sinks lined up along the walls. Little disposable hand brushes and antiseptic soap were there for hands, fingernails and arms. The water turns off automatically after the prescribed, timed scrub and we proceed, a little uncertain, through yet another wide, heavy door. This is a new world. We hear whishing, whirring and beeping noises. We see bright lights and suited-up people on tall stools quietly focused on charts and monitors. The NICU (Neonatal Intensive Care Unit) at Emanuel Hospital in Portland is a place of healing, hope, bonding and joy. For many, it is also a place of worry, fear, loss and sadness. All of those emotions became part of our daily lives during our month of keeping vigil over Vivian, our first grandchild.

Our son, Jonathan, and his wife Cristy had taken their time in planning their new family carefully. College years had certain pressures, followed by time and energy put into new jobs. Jonathan taught inner city, at-risk high school kids—high stress, but rewarding. Cristy worked with a company that developed neonatal test equipment—a chemistry/engineering/troubleshooting job with a fast pace. Jonathan and Cristy are great outdoors and sports enthusiasts with a circle of close friends, so life was busy and enjoyable.

One evening, Jonathan called and said, "Can you guys come to dinner tomorrow night?"

We said, "Sure, that would be great." We wondered what was going on since it was a weeknight and everyone got up pretty early.

The next evening there were six of us: myself and my husband Gary, our daughter Julia and her husband Todd, our son Jonathan and his wife Cristy. Jonathan cooked which was not unusual. He likes to cook. During the evening though, Jonathan called us to order and said, "Cristy and I just wanted to announce that we are expecting a baby." Boy, what excitement! We had wondered if it would ever happen. After 11 years, the announcement of Cristy's pregnancy was very exciting. She and Jonathan had big grins and enjoyed the moment, but Cristy was a bit pale and quiet. She was suffering the nausea of early pregnancy.

They began to "prepare the nest." Jonathan made a job change to allow more flexibility in his schedule to be a "hands-on" Dad. Cristy was a bit nervous about the response to her pregnancy at work, but when she told her boss, the owner of the company, his response was, "Astoria Pacific is going to have a baby!" He started making plans that would allow telecommuting and other changes in her schedule.

Gary and I knew they would both be wonderful parents. As soon as Cristy felt the new life inside her, she had a name—Vivian, meaning "life." This baby was quick and active and on the move.

One afternoon they came by for a late lunch. It was Saturday and Jonathan had been working on a fixer-upper house they had bought. Cristy was with him, mostly resting and lying down. The nausea had continued even after the first trimester and cramping and some bleeding had been a problem as well. As soon as they came into our house, Cristy asked, "Can I use your computer?" Pretty soon we realized that she was very upset and she said, "We need to go!" She believed from her research on the web that she was starting labor—15 weeks before her due date.

On their way home they called their very experienced midwife. She stayed in close contact because of some of the difficulties Cristy had experienced and met them at their house. She examined Cristy and quickly said, "You're going to the hospital now." She called Emanuel Hospital in Portland to let them know Cristy was coming in.

Cristy was put on medication to stop labor, but on her third day in the hospital, August 6, 2004, Vivian made her dramatic appearance. She weighed in at 1 pound 10 ounces. She was 11 inches long and her little head was about the size of a lemon.

The gamut of emotions that ran through me that day was more extreme than I had ever experienced. Cristy's family is a strong unit, and her mother, sister and aunt were in the delivery room along with Jonathan and me. Outside of my own two children, this was the first time I had been present at a birth. The excitement of seeing that little person make her entrance to this world was so great.

In the same hour, Jonathan, Gary, and I stood in the hallway with the hospital chaplain, who is a personal friend of our family. We discussed together the dangers of such an early birth. A doctor had read the statistics to our family the night before—the likelihood of disabilities of all kinds. They were mental retardation, loss of hearing, loss of sight, respiratory and neurological issues that crippled permanently and numerous complications that were fatal.

As we talked with the chaplain in the hallway, Jonathan said, "I believe that all things work together for good when we love God. Cristy and I have talked about this and we are committed to Vivian, no matter what. We know it could be tough, but we will face it together."

Hope After the Death of a Child

I was awe-stricken by this. He was making his statement of faith. He was verbalizing something that he might have to look back on to carry him through some very hard times. I was so proud of the two of them, but also very concerned. I have read the statistics of divorce in families that faced hardships of this kind, and I've had strong, committed friends who were among them. I have also known some who faced these things with grace and courage and their child became such a blessing, bringing their family closer together. I also struggled with what Vivian may have to endure.

In spite of this, we knew of babies born even earlier than Vivian that made it and lived totally normal lives. For my own thinking at that time, I chose the path of faith in God and prayer for her normal development. There was such excitement and I so enjoyed that part of the experience. I chose not to dwell on any gloomy prospects for her future. Jonathan and Cristy were going to need strength and encouragement from those they were with. I held on to the hope that Vivian would come through with flying colors. After all, her name meant "life," and that is what I prayed for—LIFE!

That began our four-week vigil as a family. Jonathan and Cristy took leave from their work and were with Vivian night and day, taking turns at timed intervals when they could change her diaper and take her temperature. Friends from Christ Community Church had a family member who loaned them a camper to park at the hospital so they could have a place to rest.

Cristy was able, because of her work with neonatal equipment, to have a fuller awareness of Vivian's condition and she hardly left her side.

I picture her still, brooding over Vivian's little corner of the room, watching the monitors, listening to the noises and speaking to the nurse about little changes.

Vivian's existence was totally in the isolette with the cover on. She was very sensitive to touch and any distraction tired her. Her eyes were not open yet and she had a protective mask to keep out any light. The kids drew little eyes and eyelashes on the mask and called it her "Aspen ski mask".

She was on a respirator and all of her body functions were monitored. She was extremely wired up. With the respirator attachment to her mouth and the mask on her eyes and a number of tubes going here and there, we were unable to see how she really looked, but she had beautiful, dark, wavy hair and lovely little hands with tiny fingernails. She was perfect in every way—just so small.

Every day we were there we felt like celebrating. It was August and the sunny weather and outdoor spaces around the hospital were cheering. One of our jobs while we were at Emanuel was to see that Cristy and Jonathan were fed. They were so focused on Vivian and our wise Chaplain, Jill, instructed us to take care of them so they

Hope After the Death of a Child

could stay strong for the baby. "Bring food!" she said.

This gave us a mission and we enjoyed some close times with members of our family, Cristy's family and the kids' friends, as we shared meals together in the garden or on the large deck outside the NICU.

We celebrated when Vivian opened one eye to peep at her dad. Then a couple of days later the other eye popped open. More celebrating.

We celebrated when Cristy had the chance to hold Vivian for the first time after a couple of weeks. Vivian, with all her lines and attachments, was carefully moved to Cristy's chest—skin to skin. Vivian snuggled down and soon started making little slurping noises. Her nursing instinct was kicking in even at that stage of development. It was a brief moment, but full of tenderness and bonding for mother and baby. Vivian knew her parents' voices and would actually try to push herself up when she heard them.

Two people at a time could be in the NICU and I was enjoying my turn with Jonathan. It was time for him to change her diaper.

"Mom, do you want to help me?" he asked. Would I?! He carefully lifted her by the feet and we slipped the tiny, clean diaper under her bottom, each of us holding one side. She had the tiniest little feet and the tiniest little bottom, with her skin slipping around her like a little old person. She was not fully grown into it yet. She was light as a feather. We took the soiled diaper out from under her and set it aside to be weighed. I tucked the clean diaper between her little legs and left it loose around her. We also took her temperature. She did not like the thermometer under her arm.

That would do for now. That was about as much messing with her as we should do. Back to sleep. Time to grow.

We got to know other families who also had little ones in the NICU. It was amazing to see the courage of those who were waiting like we were. Some had large, supportive families. One mother waited alone. The father was not part of their lives. We shared with each other of the progress of our babies.

Her baby was eventually released and went home to grandma's house with her mother. We all congratulated her and were happy after seeing her go through some fearful times alone.

One large family group waited about three weeks. They were "all out" in being there for each other and had strong spiritual roots. Their baby had been full term, but something happened in delivery to cause an extreme loss of blood. He faced severe mental retardation and other problems. The father was a strong, handsome, young firefighter. He had two other young boys who were "made in his image." They were wonderful little boys and one day the five-year-old offered us his new pack of M&Ms. He had just gotten them from the vending machine. It was so sweet. We shared in the "fellowship of suffering" with that little guy.

In the end, their baby died. They were a strong testimony to the power of staying together and committing to one another for life, and they all went through that experience with a lot of grace and kindness for each other.

Another baby went on to a neighboring hospital, OHSU, for brain surgery. The young parents were alone and the mother had developed diabetes with the pregnancy. They lived in Eugene and had a very uncertain financial future, but they were committed to each other and were so hopeful for their little one. We all waited with the same hopes and concerns.

Some days were very good and then Vivian would take a dive and be hovering on the edge. She had to undergo a heart surgery and there were constant concerns of infection because of the invasiveness of all the procedures. The staff started calling her "Little Miss Vivian, the Drama Queen," because of her extreme changes.

On a Saturday morning, Cristy and Jonathan noticed that Vivian was pale and listless. She had made improvements and plans were made to take her off the respirator, but at this point she was no longer able to provide most of her own oxygen. The staff started antibiotics, suspecting infection. This was her third infection in as many weeks.

As the week progressed she became more dependent

on the respirator, but as she had grown, the tube was becoming loose. It was not giving her the help she needed and the tube needed to be replaced by a larger one. This was a problem because replacing it was not always successful on the first attempt and she would be without oxygen until the replacement was completed. What a relief when a successful replacement was done in only 40 seconds.

The relief was brief. Examination of the old tube revealed staff infection. She continued to fight for her life, but her lungs were weakening.

A few days after the decline had begun, in the early afternoon, Cristy and Jonathan called all of us to the hospital. They were both very controlled, almost like they were trying to shield us as Jonathan told us, "The doctors are saying that her PH level is dropping and that's a very bad sign. In fact, it probably means that we're losing her." Then, they left us to be close to Vivian.

They came and went a few times to check in, but there was no improvement as we spent the afternoon on the terrace. The weather was so gorgeous. The sun was shining and the terrace was beautiful and peaceful. It was a setting that encouraged hope. I was not letting go yet. She could still turn the corner and that continued to be my prayer.

Cristy's family and ours had always enjoyed a nice relationship, but in this month we had bonded in a new

HOPE AFTER THE DEATH OF A CHILD

way. As we sat together, no one really talked. We just felt like being quiet.

About 4:30 in the afternoon, Vivian's nurse came out. She said, "Would you all like to come with me?" That is when it really came home to me—we were not going to get to keep Vivian. These were her last moments on earth and we were going to share them with her and with each other.

When we came into the room, the nurse was just lifting Vivian out of her isolette. Jonathan had never yet held her so she carefully laid Vivian in his strong arms. The length of her whole body was smaller than his forearm. Another of her nurses, a kind man named Bill, was using a portable respirator to keep her breathing. After a few minutes, Jonathan and Cristy said it was time to let her go.

The respirator assembly and the tubes that had been her lifelines since birth were quickly removed. For the first time we saw her face fully.

She opened her dark eyes and seemed to look slowly around the circle of family. What was she experiencing then? Was she noticing the noise, the lights and the confusion after her quiet world? I go back to that look and her beautiful little face in my mind at times. We were saying our goodbyes to her, telling her how much we loved her, how beautiful she was. She appeared to be peaceful. She closed her eyes and seemed to rest.

Reasons for Hope

By 5:05 p.m. there were only two heartbeats per minute, and finally, no more. She died in Cristy's arms.

There are times when the best choice is to lay aside responsibility and schedules and just sit together and wait. Hope, fear, joy and sadness each took their turns visiting us as we waited together all those hours. We were bound together by all of it. In the end, our love for Vivian fell on each other and our own grief was comforted by it.

For Cristy and Jonathan, Vivian gave the gift of knowing that they were parents deep within themselves. Two years have passed now. They have spent time grieving and healing and are making plans for a family again, either through birth or adoption.

A good family is a great treasure. Our two families—Cristy's and Jonathan's—are different in a lot of ways. One way we are alike, however, is that we respect and love each other. I have never felt a sense of competition between us and I have never experienced manipulation by anyone. At a time of grief, it is so warm to be together, sharing the load and comforting one another.

Hope After the Death of a Child

I am comforted by Jesus' teaching about Heaven, a place of beauty where we will be with Him and God the Father, forever. The Bible teaches that for everyone who puts their trust in Jesus (and those too young to do so), being absent from the body is to be present with the Lord. I believe that when Vivian left us she wasn't just assimilated into some nebulous life force, or that the great little spirit we knew was snuffed out. I believe that others that I miss, my mom, my dad and Cristy's Grandpa Dick, were there to receive Vivian. I do not fully grasp or understand it because this life is all I know, but it is a great comfort. I have the hope of seeing all of them again.

There will be other children to fill our lives, but we will always remember Vivian and love her. She was our first.

2

HOPE AFTER CHILD ABUSE

Roy

The whole family was seated around the breakfast table on the apple boxes and wooden blocks that served as our chairs. Mom and Dad were quietly talking while us kids were busy eating. Before any of us realized what was happening, the quiet of the morning was shattered as Dad flew into a rage, picking up his freshly poured cup of coffee and flinging its scalding contents into my Mom's face.

The hot, steaming liquid hit her just under the chin and ran down her neck, peeling away the skin as it seeped down. Mom screamed out in surprise and pain, the baby started crying and the rest of us jumped up from the table, knocking over the seats with a loud crash. We were used to Dad's tirades, but none of us understood why he would hurt Mom like that.

Dad ran for the back door with Sis after him, pounding him on the back and yelling, "Why did you do that? You had no business throwing that hot coffee on Mom! You're just mean!" But the back door slammed shut, and Dad was gone. Sis knew it was hopeless to chase after him, but it helped release the anger she felt toward him.

He was not going to change, and we all knew he would hurt any of us that actually caught up with him.

Sis raced back to help us with Mom. As she carefully lifted the dress from Mom's body, the skin came off with it, revealing the blood vessels under the raw flesh. I could feel the hatred boiling up within me as I looked at Mom suffering so. Seeing her like this made me sick inside. All Mom had done was quietly try to talk to Dad about coming home drunk the night before and using up the recent crop money for liquor. There were bills to be paid and with winter approaching, all of us kids would need shoes to wear on our now bare feet when we went to school. But Dad did not like to be corrected in any way, so he got angry and threw the cup of coffee. I hated him for hurting Mom.

After things settled down, most of us left for school, but Sis stayed home that day to help Mom. We did not call a doctor since we couldn't afford one.

Dad was still not around when we returned from school that evening, and Mom said she had not seen him all day. We found him out in the corncrib that evening hunkered down for the night among the sacks of feed with his precious jug lying on top of him. He was pretty much out of it. We left him there without a word. Everybody pitched in and did the evening chores, milking the cows and feeding the pigs before going inside for supper.

In spite of everything he did, we could not help but

love him for he was our Dad. At times like this, though, all of us felt like beating him up, but we knew better than to actually try it. He liked to fight when he was boozed up, and when he was like that there was no telling what he might do.

Life was hard on the farm in Webster County, Georgia, where we grew up in the 1930s and '40s. At the time I came into the world in 1932, our family used the horse and wagon for transportation. Dad was working for the WPA (Works Progress Administration), the government's effort to provide work for families like ours during the depression years. Money was scarce in our household, so we all had to pitch in and work long and hard. We grew our own food (turnip greens, yams, Irish potatoes and other garden produce), which meant the garden had to be weeded and tended. But our main work was on our 100-acre farm, which was our source of income.

Since it was more important to keep the farm running than go to school and get an education, my childhood was spent putting in a good day's work on the land. We would get up before dawn to harness up the horse or mule, take them to the field and hitch them to the plow, then plow the corn and peanut fields. If we were lucky enough, we could go to school after some of the work was done. I understood how important it was to work on the farm, but I wanted to be like the other kids and go to school every day.

REASONS FOR HOPE

I wanted to go to school so badly that, sometimes, I would hide in the cornfield near the road, waiting for the bus to come by. Dad would come out with his shotgun looking for me, calling out, "Roy, you get back here! I want you to stay home and work the field today!" This was followed by a stream of curse words, tainting the fresh morning air. Then he would threaten, "I'll get even with you! You'll be back tonight."

As I peeked out through the stalks of corn where I was hiding, I would see the bus stop to pick up my younger brother and sisters. As it started moving again and lumbered down the narrow, dirt road, I would dash out from my hiding place, and the bus would stop and let me on. I would hang my head and not look at anyone, as embarrassment would creep over me. My friends never razzed me, though, and the bus driver was a neighbor who always looked out for us kids. The neighbors and the community pretty well knew about our family, and many felt sorry for us, and the conditions we had to live in. When I arrived home later, I would go straight out to the field to finish my work. Thankfully, Dad usually was not around anywhere. When he was angry, it was best just to stay out of his sight.

Beside my work in the field, I was given another important responsibility: keeping lookout while my brother, Frank, and a neighbor made moonshine. During the prohibition days, liquor could not be sold, but that did not

HOPE AFTER CHILD ABUSE

stop people like them from illegally making their own to use or sell. They had a still deep in the woods and the property owners were not even aware of what was going on back there. My job was to sit on an old stump with a shotgun across my lap to keep watch. They worked mostly at night, late in the fall. The weather was getting really chilly and my teeth would be chattering so that I could hardly sit still. It would be hours before I would hear them come out from among the trees. I knew by the way they were acting that they had been sampling some of their product. But it was a relief to see them coming so that I could run home and get under the blankets to try to warm up and get some rest before the next day started. It is amazing that we were not caught and jailed.

My dad ran the family with an iron fist. He was boss, and as soon as one of the boys in our family would get old enough to start thinking for himself and make suggestions, Dad could not take it. He had made it so hard on my older brothers, Frank and Mil, that they both left home at the same time, when they were only 16 and 18 years old. I was the next oldest boy, so a lot of the responsibility of the farm then fell on me.

The Christmas after they left was a day filled with both joy and heartache. That morning, we happened to look out the window and got the shock of our lives. Here was a pickup truck coming up the dirt road to our house. We did not usually have company, especially not on

REASONS FOR HOPE

Christmas day when most people would be with their families. Running outside to greet the pickup, we found it was our neighbor, the bus driver. He parked and began taking out all sorts of gifts and handing them to us: a football, a basketball, a ball and bat, and gloves for me and my younger brothers, Nat and Larry. He also had gifts for my sisters, Sue, Sis and Ann. It was like our own personal visit from Santa.

An even better surprise, though, was when my two older brothers appeared from around the corner of the house. We did not think our family would be together for Christmas, so we were excited to see them. As they came toward us, we all ran up to hug them when they suddenly stopped cold with fearful looks on their faces. There was Dad, staring them down with that stony glare that always meant trouble. With his raspy voice he yelled at them, "You get off this place! You're not wanted here! Stay away from here and don't come back!"

The rest of us watched with sorrow as Frank and Mil quickly turned away and started down the road. As they went, our neighbor also left without saying anything, picking them up on his way out to give them a ride to town. The day that should have been so special ended with a silent sadness in all of us.

When Dad got a job in Florida building military houses, the rest of us stayed in Georgia to run the farm. As the oldest son still at home, I became the "man of the house." Dad would come home about one weekend a month and give me instructions about what needed to be done around the farm. Mom, Sis and I kept the place running, and the younger ones did what they could. We enjoyed how peaceful it had become on the farm. The women did almost as much work as I did to get the crops in, taking care of all the cows, pigs and horses, and doing anything else that needed to be done. The work was hard and the humidity and heat just about did me in, but I was young and strong, and I learned to put in a full day's work without complaint. In a way, it felt good to know that I was helping the family and that Dad trusted me to do this.

In the fall, Dad came home for a long weekend, and the peace of our home was once again shattered. The days were getting cooler, and the sugar cane had been cut, stripped and then laid out to cure in the shade. Dad and I planned to take it to the grinder on Saturday, so I loaded the sugar cane in the wagon, piling it high above the 18-inch-tall sideboards. On Friday night, I went to bed early to prepare for the big day ahead. I was up by 4:00 the next morning, and as I was lacing up my shoes, getting ready to go out, Dad came in and said, "Roy, I'm just not feeling good this morning. You're going to have to take over for me." With that, he headed back to bed, and I put on my coat and hat and went out to take care of the job ahead. I was disappointed that I would have to do this by myself, but I was also proud that Dad would trust me with this responsibility.

I hitched the horses to the wagon, climbed up onto the pile of cane with reins in hand, and started off to the cane mill at a neighboring farm. While I was waiting my turn at the grinder, a neighbor came over to chat with me.

"Little Roy, why didn't your dad come with you?" My dad's name was Roy and I was Roy Jr., but everyone called me Little Roy.

I was too embarrassed by the truth, so I just used the same excuse that Dad had used that morning. "He's sick, so he decided to stay home."

"I bet he's been drinking again," said our neighbor.

He was right, but I did not admit it. I just looked away hoping nothing more would be said, and he knew well enough to leave it alone. It was discouraging to know that my family had that kind of reputation.

While the cane was being prepared, I sat by the warm fire where the cane juice was boiling and watched the rhythm of the grinding, letting it lull me to sleep. A horse was attached to two long poles branching out from the wheel gear that cranked the rollers, and as it walked its circuit around the mill to keep it in motion, the men poked the cane stalks between the rollers to squeeze the juice out. The juice was then carried to a huge cast-iron cauldron sunk into the ground with space for a fire underneath. I helped stoke up the fire and drank in the wonderful smell of cane juice boiling into syrup. It made for a long day, but I was so proud when I set out for home with several shiny-new, one-gallon cans of freshly cooked syrup. Little did I know what had gone on at home that day during my absence.

My younger brother, Nat, met me at the door when I arrived home, and I immediately knew something was wrong. I listened as he told me what had happened. Dad had gone into a rage again and had hit our four-year-old brother, Larry, in the face with the hot fire poker. The impact left a black mark of soot imbedded under the skin on his cheek, a mark that he would carry for the rest of his life. Nat had watched with horror as it happened, the memory marking him just as surely as the poker had marked Larry. With every scar, our family was torn further apart and more bitterness grew toward our father.

I was tired from the long day, and coming home to this story just added to my weariness. I headed for bed to try to blot out the heart-pain and the memory of what happened to my poor little brother, covering my head as though this would hide me and help me forget. I had been so proud of the work I did that day, but there had been no greeting at the door that night for a job well done. The next day, Dad headed back to Florida without a word of praise for me.

My older brother, Frank, had gone into the service as World War II started, and after the war ended, he came home to work the farm with Dad. They even invested in more horses and farming equipment, but things did not go as planned. We soon found out that Frank had learned the ways of drinking and partying in the Army, and now he could drink as much as Dad. Between the two of them, it was constant arguing and turmoil. Eventually, Dad got fed up with it and returned to his old job in Florida, leaving Frank and me to bring in the crops that year. We decided to use the crop money so that Mom and us kids could go down to Florida, and then Frank planned to return to Georgia and run the farm.

Later that fall, we packed up and headed for Florida, along with Frank's friend, Bill, who let us use his truck. As we headed down the road with the back of that truck packed to overflowing with furniture and kids sticking out at different angles, we looked just like the Beverly Hillbillies. I felt kind of embarrassed that anyone would see us.

When we arrived at the address Dad had given us, we were excited as we pulled up in front of a beautiful house. But as Dad came out of the garage by the side of the house, our hearts sank—we realized this was where he was living, in the garage, not in the nice, spacious house. This tight space is where he was expecting Mom, Sue, Ann, Nat, Larry, baby sister, Martha, and myself to move in with him.

Dad was happy to see us and was in a really good

mood that day, and we were all happy to see him, too. Later that afternoon, as we were unloading the truck, a young boy about my age was standing across the street watching what was happening at his neighbor's place. When Dad saw him, he called me over. "Roy," he said, "see that boy over there with the blue shirt on? I want you to go over and beat him up. He's always watching me and sticking his nose into my business. Just go on over and take care of him." I was stunned. "Why, Dad?"

"I just don't like him," he answered.

I looked at my dad and said, "I can't do that. I don't even know him. If I'm going to live here, he just may become my best friend. I'm not going to beat him up." Dad looked at me with disgust and walked off. I so wanted his approval, but this was wrong, and I was not about to do what he wanted me to do. I could tell that I had become a disappointment to him. I always tried to do what Dad told me, so he probably thought I would do anything he wanted, and now, here I was, refusing to do as I was told.

Later that evening, I overheard a conversation between Dad, Frank and Bill. They did not know I could hear them, and even if they had, I am not sure it would have mattered.

"Frank, when you go on back to the farm, I want you to take that #*!#%# Roy back with you. I don't want him around here because he won't do anything I say." My heart sank and tears welled up in my eyes. I felt utterly and totally rejected. Why didn't Dad want me to live with my own family? He didn't even want me around! I was having a hard time getting a grip on this, and more bitterness crept into my heart. "I'll show him," I thought. "Someday, I'll grow up and be somebody, and he'll see what I can do. Then he'll like me and wish he'd been nicer to me." I was not going to be a drunkard and fight all the time like he did. I just knew that there had to be a better way to live than this, but how would I ever find it?

Outwardly, however, I said nothing. I did not let them know that I overheard the conversation, and I hid my feelings about it. No one was ever going to see how that had hurt me. When it was time to go back to the farm, I headed back to Georgia with Frank and Bill. But as we were driving along, I soon found out that Georgia was not their final destination. They had come up with a new plan. Once we got to the farm, they would get rid of stuff there that needed attention and then head for California. Bill had gotten married while serving in the Navy there and now had a wife and son waiting for him.

My thoughts were really in turmoil now as I thought about their plan. I had expected to see the rest of my family when they returned to the farm before long, but now we were planning to be gone from there, way off somewhere else. It felt like my world was falling apart. But I had little choice. I had to do as I was told.

The more I thought about it, though, the more excited

HOPE AFTER CHILD ABUSE

I became about the trip. I had seen pictures of mountains and other beautiful scenery in magazines, and now I was going to get to see the world. I was starting to feel more grown up, so I told myself it would not be so bad not to be with Mom and the family. The bottom line, however, was that I had no choice except to go.

When we arrived at the farm, we gave away our horses, cows, pigs and the corn that was still in the fields, and we told the neighbors to help themselves to the rest of the farm implements. We still needed to settle up our account at the country store that supplied our needs during the year, so Frank went into town and talked the store clerk into marking the account "paid in full," promising that he would be back to pay it. However, Frank never intended to make good on that promise, a decision that later came back to haunt him. I felt really bad about what he did because I knew it was not right, but he was my older brother, and I had no say in the matter.

Late one night, we locked up the old house and barns and left under the cover of darkness so we would not get caught. On the journey westward near Columbus, Georgia, we stopped briefly where Sis and her husband lived. She and Bud came out to greet us. I was in the back of the truck with our belongings, the mattress that served as our hotel and my dog. I did not get out of the truck so that Frank would think I was still asleep, but I was awake and listening. Peeking through the cracks between the boards that made up the sides of the truck, I watched the scene in the front yard and picked up on every word being spoken. I was shocked as I heard what Frank had to say about me.

"We're heading out to California, but we don't know what to do with Little Roy. Dad didn't want him in Florida with them. Can I leave him here with you?"

"You know we don't have our own farm here, we're only sharecropping," Bud replied. "We hardly earn enough to take care of our own family, and some of that money has to pay for our equipment. And we have a new baby on the way. I'm sorry, but we can't afford to take him."

As I overheard the conversation, I felt the same terrible rejection as I had that day in Florida. It was a feeling that stayed with me for a long time and affected me deeply. My dad did not want me around, and my sister and brother-in-law could not have me staying with them, so Frank was stuck with me, even though he did not like it. No one in my family seemed to want me.

At least Bill, my brother's friend, stuck up for me. "It's going to be all right," he told Frank. "Don't worry about it." But that did not help to soothe the ache in my heart.

As I stayed hidden in the back of the truck, I wondered, "What's going to happen to me going off into this unknown?" I felt homeless, helpless and hopeless. I was only 14 years old, and no one in my family wanted me.

HOPE AFTER CHILD ABUSE

To say the least, it was not a happy trip for me, knowing what I knew. What could have been an exciting new adventure seemed to drag on without end, just like those long nights in the cold forest guarding the moonshine still.

Our destination was a fruit ranch near Yuba City, California, where Bill's father-in-law was ranch foreman. But shortly after our arrival, we found out that we had not completely left our past behind us. The incident at the store in Georgia caught up with us when a notice from the Georgia district attorney's office arrived for my brother. His options were either jail or military service, so he chose to go back into the military

With Frank's departure, I was now all alone. This was new to me. I had always had some family around, and though much of that time was not pleasant, at least I had felt some measure of security. But now my new surroundings were strange to me, and I felt there was no one I could go to for help in sorting out my life.

Bill was kind enough to let me stay on with him for a while, so I was able to work part-time and continue on with my schooling. We settled near Sutter City, where I did several kinds of jobs. Back then, people like me served as the migrant workers, working in whatever fields needed extra hands from one season to the next. In the fall, I would pick olives, tie burlap bags as they were filled with kidney beans, or man a rice-harvesting machine. In the spring, I would thin the peaches and later pick them or gather and bag nuts as they were shaken from the trees. I also did some work for a local farmer before and after school each day, irrigating his alfalfa fields and operating his crawler tractor. The fields I worked in now were much larger than our small farm in Georgia; often three or four times the size. I felt lost in the midst of it all. So many changes had taken place so quickly in my life. I felt like it was just yesterday that things were so very different.

When I was not working, I had no adult guidance so I ran with some unruly kids that I met at school. We would hang around in the pool halls, go to football games, or steal watermelons from the fields. One night, we drove way out into the country where I knew there were watermelons being grown and I was going to show my companions how brave I was.

Carefully and quietly, I crept into the field and located the melons. I hoisted two of them under my arms and headed out, running as fast as I could back to the car.

Suddenly, I was thrown backwards and had the wind knocked out of me. In my running, I had not noticed the clothesline strung across my path, and down I went. The watermelons got crushed, so I left them there as I scurried back to the car. With the dogs from the farm quickly catching up with me, I jumped in the car and we peeled out before we were caught. If the farmer saw us stealing from his field, we might have been shot on sight.

When we did manage to steal some watermelons, we used them for pranks. One Friday, on a warm summer evening, we drove by a church with its doors wide open. They must have been holding a prayer meeting. The long aisle down the center of the sanctuary was beckoning to us, so I snuck up to the doors and rolled a watermelon as hard as I could down the aisle. We lingered long enough to watch it split open as it hit the altar, but then we bolted before anyone could come after us. It was disruptive and irreverent, but we had not been raised in church, so we didn't think of it in any special, sacred way. We did not care what we did or how it affected other people, as long as we were not caught.

Eventually, it was necessary for me to set out on my own in order to have an income, a place to stay and food to eat. I had worked on a certain ranch before so I went to the owner and asked him for a job. He put me to work for $60 a month, plus room and board. It was not a lot, but at least I had a roof over my head and food to eat. My room was a spot in the tool shed where they would work on the farming equipment. There were all sorts of tools and equipment throughout the place, so we built a wall, creating a small section in the corner which was to be my room. It had a small cot for a bed. It was not much, but for now it was home. One day, I was working with Warren Earl, the owner's brother-in-law, when he asked me if

REASONS FOR HOPE

I would like to go to church with him the next Sunday. I was curious about church so I agreed to go with him. I did not know what to expect since I had never been to church before.

Warren picked me up that Sunday evening and we headed to a small town nearby called Live Oak. The church was a quaint little white building situated among houses. I was able to meet some of the people there that first night. They seemed to be like a big family, one that really cared about each other. The folks were so warm and friendly; these were the kind of people I wanted to get to know. The teenagers who were my age, about 15, just accepted me as if they had always known me. These kids were so different than any I had known before. For one thing, they dressed nicely, but it was more than that. They really liked each other and were able to have lots of fun without causing trouble, unlike my friends and me. My aching heart longed to have a life like these church kids. I was reaching out to them and they were reaching out to me.

I really enjoyed spending time with the people at church, so when I was invited to go back again the next week, I eagerly accepted. On my third visit, there was a special speaker, and his message really caught my attention. He talked about sin in our lives, and he told us of a heavenly Father who loved us and whom we could get to know personally. This was exactly what I longed for in my life. I was so in need of a father who loved me, who would forgive me of everything I had ever done and accept me, just the way that I was. When the speaker called for us to come up front, I, along with a number of the other teens, ran to the front of the church to pray. I wanted to know this Father's love, and that night I asked Jesus to forgive me of all my sins and wrongdoings and come into my life so I could become part of God's family.

Not long after that was my 16th birthday. My family had never celebrated birthdays, so I thought nothing special of the day and went about my work as usual. Little did I know that this day would be a very special one after all, and that I would be receiving a gift that I would treasure forever! We were working on building a large new barn for the ranch, and I had not noticed anything unusual as I did my work. But as we were finishing up for the day, my boss, Mr. Gatchell, pulled me aside.

"Roy, I want you to go down the road and pick up that little war refugee girl. She'll be joining us for dinner tonight."

The young lady he spoke of was from Estonia, and she lived with her family in an outbuilding on a nearby ranch. I did as I was asked and when we returned, I noticed several more cars parked by the barn than when I had left. There were people going into the new building, so when I recognized one of my school friends coming out, I went up to him and asked what was going on. He said, "Come on, let's see." As he led me through the door, I could hardly believe what was happening: everyone started singing "Happy Birthday" to me. This was the first birthday party I had ever had, and I did not even realize they knew it was my birthday. There were tables set up with food and drinks, and hay bales were placed around the sides of the building to sit on. They had made room for a barn dance and there was a live country-western band. Some of my classmates from Sutter High School were there, and altogether there must have been almost 60 people.

Just the thoughtfulness of the celebration was enough of a gift, but that night was also special in another way. Mr. and Mrs. Gatchell knew of the change in my life since I had starting attending church. Even though they did not attend church much, they made a special presentation to me—a brand new Bible with my name engraved in gold letters on the cover. I was overwhelmed by this gift, and my voice was really choked up as I tried to tell them how much it meant to me.

"This is the first birthday party I've ever had, and I've never had a Bible before," I told them, hardly able to keep the tears back. Receiving that book was the next step in getting to know God as my loving Father, and that day marked the beginning of my love for God's word. That Bible became my constant companion, and despite its bulk, it even accompanied me through the Korean War. I still have it to this day.

About a year and a half later, the time came for me to move on. I had made good friends here and attended church with them, so moving away meant that for the first time I was on my own in my new Christian lifestyle. It felt like I was moving away from my family for the second time. Bill and some other men I knew had found good work at the Redwood Saw Mills in northern California, and I set out to join them. I packed what little I owned and took a Greyhound bus to San Francisco and then on up Highway 101 to Smith River. I got a job as a choker setter on the night shift, manning heavy cables to pull the logs into the mill. It was hard and dirty work and the accommodations were not much cleaner. The mill camp where I lived consisted of two rows of Army tents with wooden floors and a muddy street in between. I did go to church there a couple of times, but it just was not the same as what I had experienced in Live Oak. Eventually, I just stopped going. I still had my Bible, but I no longer had the encouragement and support of friends, so it was harder to make the right choices.

When the superintendent from that mill left to go to Klamath, a lot of the workers, including myself, went with him to the new job and location. I was no longer going to church, and I began to feel dissatisfied with my life. One night, I was walking through the rain to meet some friends at the pool hall, and as I passed by a puddle, something caught my attention. There was a card floating in the water, and I felt compelled to reach down and pick it up. The paper read, "Welcome to Klamath Assembly of God Church."

That struck a chord in my heart. I did not actually know what kind of church I had gone to before, but this sounded familiar. I felt a tugging inside, like God had put that card in my path on purpose and was trying to tell me something. Was this really a sign from God, or was I just making too much of it? I stood there in the rain for a moment, thinking this through, and then I made an important decision. I went into the pool hall and told my friends, "I'm sorry, guys, but I can't play pool tonight." Then I showed them the card I had found and told them, "I'm going to church tomorrow morning!"

I really wanted to go to church again, but it was a lonely decision because everyone else I knew was sleeping in or kicking back on Sunday morning. It felt awkward to go alone, but I got up the courage and went. When I opened the door of the church that next morning, I was quite surprised to find that there were people there with whom I worked at the mill! I saw the mill electrician and Lorin Short, the sawyer at the mill. It turns out Lorin was also the Youth Pastor at the church. I found new companionship at work, as each morning at break, three or four of us workers would join Lorin in the electricians' shack for a word from the Bible and prayer.

Lorin and I grew to be very good friends, and he was an important example of the Christian life, encouraging me, teaching me and praying with me. During the time I lived and worked in Klamath, God really did some important things in my life. I was learning to live the way God wanted me to live and to trust Him in everything. For the first time in my life, I had developed a relationship with a loving Father. I was no angel and I still had some rough edges, but God found me where I was and began to work in my life.

The changes in my life were evident to other people as well, and my integrity and good work ethic earned me the favor of my managers. At only 18 years old, I was offered a job as a lumber grader, one of the highest paying positions at the mill.

A couple years later, in June of 1952, I experienced another important change in my life. My brother, Mil, had landed a job in Portland, Oregon, and I planned to take a week of vacation and go visit him there before heading to a Christian retreat camp just north of Salem for the rest of the week. On Sunday morning, when I arrived in Portland, I took a taxi to the place where Mil lived and worked. He was not there, but someone gave me the phone number to his girlfriend's home. I called and talked to her mother, and when she heard that I was Mil's brother, she invited me to dinner. When I arrived at her house, I was greeted with a pleasant surprise. Mil's girlfriend had a sister, a beautiful young woman named Arlene.

During the next three months, I frequently made the long trip up from Klamath to visit Arlene, back in the days before the interstate highway system, driving the 1947 four-door Studebaker that I had bought on that first visit. It did not take long for me to decide to quit my job and move to Portland. While we courted, Arlene and I made our mutual interest in God the center of our relationship. We attended Sunday church services mornings and evenings, as well as special youth meetings on Saturday nights.

It was after one of those Saturday night meetings that we sat in the parking lot in my old Studebaker and talked about the call for repentance that we had heard at the meeting. That night, Arlene opened a new chapter in her relationship with God by asking forgiveness for all her past sins and wrongdoings and asking Jesus to be her Savior. A couple of months later, we were married. I had plenty of anxiety about my new role as a husband since I had not grown up with a positive example, but God had blessed me with a Christian wife, and the lessons I had learned through my Christian friends and through the Bible guided me in how to properly love and respect her. Together, we built a good Christian home, and we were eventually blessed with three children who have grown

Hope After Child Abuse

up to serve the Lord.

Soon after we married, I met with a new challenge to my Christian commitment; the Korean War was going on, and I was drafted into the Army. I left my new wife and headed to Camp Roberts in California for basic training before being shipped out. Nearly all the guys I took training with were being sent to the frontline units. Arlene and I were concerned about me coming home safely, but we knew that prayer changes things, so we asked God to protect me. In answer to our prayers, my orders were changed, and I was sent to an engineering company that was building roads and a prison camp and running supply trucks to the frontlines.

The first 18 months of our married life were spent apart while I was stationed in Korea. Arlene and I learned, through our experience, that military wives are also heroes, as it is difficult to be alone and to be supportive of the one in danger. That time was a test of our faithfulness and our commitment to each other and our commitment to the Lord. But He never left us and helped us walk victoriously through the challenges. We continually thanked God for watching over us while we were apart and bringing us safely back together.

When I returned home from Korea, I was concerned that the time away would make it difficult for me to find work. I had grown up in a home where money was scarce, and I wanted to provide a better life for my own family. But God blessed me with good opportunities. My old job was waiting for me in a plywood mill, and before long, I started an apprenticeship learning about cabinets, fixtures and millwork under the G. I. Bill. I was trained to be a good craftsman, and I also gained experience in home remodeling through the company for which I worked. Eventually I opened my own business doing finish carpentry work, earning jobs in some expensive homes around the Portland Metropolitan Area. I know that God is to be thanked for the talent and opportunities I have been given over the years.

After awhile, my work brought in enough money that I could afford to send some of it back to Georgia to help my family. My parents had moved back to the farm in Georgia, and some of my younger siblings still lived with them. When I had first left home for California, I was determined to earn enough money to help them if I could. Only later did I learn that Dad had not told the rest of the family about the checks I had sent, but spent the money on booze for himself. Thankfully, when we found out what was happening, I was able to get the checks to my mom instead, but it hurt to know that Dad could throw away my hard-earned money like that. I had seen over the years how God had changed my own life, but I still longed to see Him change the heart of my dad.

Sometime after the birth of our first two children, Arlene and I received a telegram from Georgia: "Dad had a heart attack. Please come." This was in April of 1959 when flying was still very expensive, so we decided to take the train and headed out right away. Ironically, we arrived in Columbus, Georgia, in the middle of Hurricane Arlene. We rented a car and drove through the storm to the hospital so I could see my dad that very day. He did not know I was coming, and I had no idea what to expect when I got there or how he would receive me. I just knew I had to see him.

I will never forget the image of my father lying there attached to all kinds of tubes and wires, his face pale and so much older than I remembered him. Nor will I forget how his eyes lit up when he saw us. In spite of everything he had done over the years, he was still my father, and I felt a deep love for him. I had long ago learned to forgive him for the way he had broken my heart and hurt the people I loved. I did not know how much time he might have left, and I was anxious to share with him the same peace I had found in my own life.

The next day, we again went to see him, and this time I took my Bible with me. We had been praying for an opportunity to speak to him about the condition of his heart—not physically, but spiritually—so we knew that God was directing our conversation that day.

"Dad, how is it with you?" I asked. "Are you on speaking terms with the Lord?"

"I sure hope so," he answered.

REASONS FOR HOPE

"Dad, would you like to know so?"

"I sure would."

The next few minutes brought a miracle that I never thought would happen. I saw my dad, this hard, mean man, now humbled and crying out to God. Arlene and I shared the good news with him, telling him how God so loved the world that He gave His only son, so that whoever believes in Him will not perish but gain eternal life. I then put my father's glasses on him so he could read aloud the words of salvation found in the Bible. That day, Dad asked for forgiveness and invited Jesus into his life, and we joined with him in a prayer to our heavenly Father.

But the real miracle is what followed that day. Dad lived for another eight months, and from that point on, there was no more drinking, no more cursing and no more fits of rage toward Mom and the family. That simple prayer had changed him, and because of that, I will forever carry with me the memories of my father as an upright and loving man. If God could change the heart of my dad, the hardest man I have ever known, then I know that God can change anyone.

HOPE AFTER CHILD ABUSE

In closing, I want to speak to my dad:

> *"Dad, when we meet in heaven, you may ask me, 'Son, why did you tell all those people how bad I was?' I'll have to tell you, Dad, I just wanted them to know how far-reaching God's love and grace are. We love you, Dad. We know you did the best you could for us. Times were hard in those days, and we forgave you a long time ago."*
>
> — Little Roy and the rest of the Witt family

3

HOPE FOR A NEW IDENTITY

JAMIE

Bam! Bam! Bam!
I had no idea who might be pounding so hard on my front door. If they did not stop, they might break it down.

"I'm coming, I'm com—"

I had not reached the doorknob yet when the door burst open in my face. Before I could understand what was happening, several cops were pointing guns at me.

"Freeze! Put your hands on top of your head and lay down on the floor, ma'am!"

"Mommy, mommy!" From my position on the floor, I could not turn to see my daughter, but I could hear her panicked cries. I could not help her because I still did not understand what was going on.

"Mommy, mommy, I'm scared!"

"Can I please be with my daughter?"

"Ma'am, stay on the floor!"

"MOMMY!"

I could not believe this was happening to me. I knew I was involved with something illegal, but I didn't really believe I would be caught. Was I going to prison this time? If I did, what would happen to my daughter? What would become of both of us now?

In that horrible moment, I saw my whole life laid out before my eyes. How did it get to this point?

My childhood had not been exactly perfect. My parents divorced when I was young, and my mom had to work a lot to take care of my older sister and me. Most of the time the two of us were all that each other had, so my sister practically raised me. Without much adult supervision, I was able to get involved in the wrong crowd early on. By seventh grade, I was partying a lot, drinking and smoking weed with my friends. When I was 15, I dropped out of school and moved into my own apartment. I kept trying to go back to school but just could not finish.

In order to support my unemployed boyfriend, Josh, and myself, I got a job at a pizza parlor. When the paycheck was not enough, I resorted to stealing money from the cash register. I did not intend to become a thief, but stealing became so easy and even necessary—if I did not bring home any money, my boyfriend would beat me. When I was fired from the pizza parlor, I got a job at a convenience store and fell into the same pattern. I became more creative in my theft and made out a money order to myself, but I felt guilty and decided to give it back. But the store pressed charges anyway. I guess this was the beginning of my criminal career.

My relationship with my family was no better than my career path. I was stealing not only from my jobs, but also from my mother, and she tried to press charges against me. My parents hated my boyfriend because he beat me, but also because he was black and I am white. When I became pregnant, that only upset my parents more. They wanted me to have an abortion, but I refused.

"Jamie, how can you raise a kid with a guy like that? You say that you love him, but you keep letting him hurt you. Is that how he shows his love for you, by beating you? If you have a baby with him, you're going to ruin the rest of your life."

"Dad, he doesn't mean to hurt me. He just gets upset and loses control sometimes. But I know he loves me. I can't leave him, and I'm not getting rid of our baby."

"Then there's nothing more I can do for you. Get out of my house, Jamie. I don't ever want to see you again."

I could never admit it to my family, but the violence did not stop after I got pregnant. Josh would accuse me of cheating on him and said that the baby was not his. He would hit me in the stomach to get back at me, even though he said that he loved me and did not want to hurt me. It is a complete miracle that the baby lived through that, but she was born beautiful and healthy.

At only 18 years old, I was a brand new mom. After Alexis was born, the three of us moved in with Josh's mom. I finally went back to school and we lived on welfare. My boyfriend continued to abuse me but, thankfully, he never hurt the baby. The last straw was a year later when I had to go to high school graduation with a black eye. I had had enough, so I took Alexis and moved back in with my mom.

When I left Josh I became my father's daughter again. I would go to his house and try to spend some time with him to rebuild our relationship, but it did not last. One day we got into an argument and he yelled at me, "The only reason you even come over here is to get a free babysitter so you can just sit around and do whatever you want!" I was devastated at his accusation and left in a rage.

I was angry at the world by now. Nobody believed in me and I did not know who I was anymore. I needed to prove everyone wrong. Most of all, I was very angry with Josh for all he had put me through. The only good thing in my life was my beautiful and perfect baby girl.

I finally ended up in an apartment with my mom living with me part of the time and helping me with the rent. I had gotten a job as a receptionist, and I was proud of my work because I no longer needed to steal. I was away from Josh and did not have him criticizing me for how I looked, so I started eating more and ended up weighing 200 pounds. But things were better than they had been, so I felt happy.

Hope For A New Identity

I started going out to bars a lot and getting in touch with old friends, especially one I used to hang out with in junior high school. When I saw the life she was now living, it was unbelievable to me what a mess she had become. She was doing meth and would borrow money from me to buy diapers for her baby because she had spent everything on drugs. I had seen my sister get involved with drugs when we were younger and the struggle she went through when she put herself through rehab. Watching my friend, I thought, "There is no way I will ever do that. It's just wrong!" Famous last words.

Soon after, I went out on a date with a guy who offered me some meth. I gave in and tried it, and from that moment on I was hooked. This turned out to be a quick way to lose the extra weight and give me lots of energy. Since I only used it on the weekends, I convinced myself that I could control the habit and so it was okay.

What I didn't realize is that I was not in control of the drugs; they had taken control over me. Suddenly I was angry at everyone again and constantly fighting with my mom and everyone else. I could not pay for an apartment, so I was moving from place to place with different friends and relatives until I wore out my welcome. At one point, I moved in with a friend's mom who was also a meth addict and I would get the meth for her. The arrangement worked great for me until it blew up in my face when she accused me of cheating her.

"Where is the rest of it, Jamie?"

"What do you mean? It's all there."

"No, it isn't! You should've been able to score twice as much with the money I gave you!"

"This is all I could get!"

"I don't believe you! You're a liar and a cheater! Give me the rest now!"

"I swear there is no more!"

"Liar! I want you out of my house!"

Once again, my daughter and I were homeless and had to stay with another friend until I could find something else for us. But I was determined to make a future for myself, so I started to attend Concord Career College to be a dental assistant. I was trying to do it all—work a full-time job, go to school full-time, run a morning paper route and raise my daughter, but I just could not do it. My job is what suffered the consequences, and as I was trying to figure out how Alexis and I were going to make it, I was offered a new opportunity to make some money. This is when the real trouble began.

A "friend" of mine introduced me to identity theft. I was doing a lot of meth, and this seemed to be a good way to get some money both to support my addiction and to pay the rent. We would find people to cash checks for us in exchange for a cut of the profit. This seemed to be the solution to all of my problems, and life was great for a while. I had lost weight because of the meth, I could

Hope For A New Identity

finally afford an apartment and a car and I was on a constant high. I felt like I finally had everything I wanted, and I could prove to my family that I did not need their help.

But the run of luck could not last forever. Eventually, we got caught for cashing false checks. This time, we got off easy because the checks were under $750 and so it was considered a misdemeanor. Just getting arrested, though, was enough to scare me.

"There's no way I'm ever going to do this again," I vowed, just like I had vowed never to get involved with drugs.

As the money ran low again, I could not afford daycare for Alexis, so she would spend the week with Josh's mom, and I would see her on the weekends. I missed my baby girl and I started to become depressed. To make matters worse, my sister was getting married and had not asked me to be in the wedding. I wanted to get my thoughts straight and decided to write a journal.

> *"Happiness to me is a job leading into my lifetime career, a beautiful house to live in, a husband, Alexis happy and loved and never without, true and real friends, fun in whatever I may do, happiness, complete and utter happiness, money and love.*
>
> *"I need to let all of my friends, my fam-*

ily and Alexis know I have been doing a lot of illegal things, like using 'a little' drugs (a lot really) and cashing checks. People may think I get a rush with the money in my hand, but I can't stand the fact of how I am getting money to make it. I feel like the world's biggest low life. I don't even like myself as a person anymore. I just don't know how to get on track, and that's not a cop-out. I know I need to work everyday, go to school and take care of my daughter. If it was only that easy. I lost my job because I couldn't pay for rent and daycare at the same time. Not to mention utilities, car payment, loan payments, phone bill, food, gas and clothes for Alexis. I tried to budget spending money. I can't afford it, being a single mom with no help from anyone.

"I am grown, it was my choice to have Alexis and I am never going to get anywhere. If I hadn't kept Alexis, I would probably be dead by the hands of her father. So, I thank God that my child was born . . . Alexis should not have been born due to all the abuse and stress my body went through during the pregnancy. Alexis is the only thing that makes my life worth anything, so I

HOPE FOR A NEW IDENTITY

owe it to her to give her a good life, unlike mine. I just can't seem to do it right. Please God, let me have something, anything. I am just so tired."

I never told anyone I was doing meth, but I think they all knew. I went to my sister's wedding really high. I was skinny—no, not skinny—scrawny, grossly scrawny. It was hard for me to understand why she did not want me to be a part of her special day. That really hurt me to the core.

The vicious cycle continued with me getting evicted once again, having to quit college and moving in with my mom in Astoria, Oregon. I cut back on the drug use, mainly because my suppliers were in the Portland Metro area. Once again, Mom and I did not get along, so I moved back to Beaverton. When I was approved for section 8 housing, I moved to Tigard and picked up where I had left off. I started college again, this time to be an accountant. But I was also going out to bars and doing and selling drugs. I had my own place and a car. The pendulum had swung my way again, and I was back on top.

When Alexis was about five, I decided to move to another apartment in Beaverton, which is where I met Teri. We became good friends and I soon found out what she was into: ID theft. Even though I had sworn never to get involved with this again, I needed a way to support my daughter and myself, and this was an easy way to make good money. Teri was into this more heavily than my previous friends had been, and she assured me that if we did it right, we would not be caught. So she taught me the finer details of ID theft and we became partners in crime.

With a computer, scanner, printer and the right software, I had everything I needed. I sat at home and made the IDs, while Teri would go to stores to use them. I told myself that what I was doing was not really wrong because I was not the one using them to get cash. With the money I earned from this, I thought I was finally happy. I was shopping every day and still going to school. I had grants and loans for school and would have been fine financially, but this was my spending cash and drug money.

Because I was spending my money on the wrong things, I tried to pay an $800 electric bill with a bad check one month and had my power turned off. I had to depend on other people again, and I asked my neighbors, Cathy and Carrie, if I could take showers at their place. As I spent more time over there, their little brother asked Alexis if she wanted to go to church with them. I saw this as an opportunity for some time to myself and told her she could go. They asked me also, but I was not interested.

Cathy and I became friends first and I would often go

HOPE FOR A NEW IDENTITY

next door just to sit and talk with her. Eventually, Carrie and I also became good friends. I was amazed at the kindness of these girls. I was sure they had seen all the people going in and out of my apartment, and yet they still let me come into their home and accepted me for who I was. I really admired them. Carrie was only about 20 at the time, and I could not believe what a strong woman she was. I just kept thinking, "Wow, she's really got it together!"

Carrie never judged me. She was always herself around me. She knew what was going on and she was still my friend. Carrie would talk to me about God and she never changed. That was the best part—she never changed. Whenever I asked her a question or told her something, it was always the same answer. She was a good, Christian woman. Cathy and Carrie were always there for me. Their church even donated money to me when my electricity was turned off. Alexis loved them and that was important. *They were always happy and I wanted that!*

As for me, I needed to stay high to feel happy. I was doing drugs all the time now. I kept my stash in my bedroom, where Alexis would not see it, but I imagine she knew something was going on.

Teri and I were successful with ID theft for about two and a half years. Then Teri got caught, and I found out what a good and faithful friend she was—she immediately ratted me out. Not only did she turn me in, but she was apparently doing other things at my house while I was at school so that I would be the one held responsible.

That day when the SWAT team burst through my front door, I did not know what to think. They had their guns drawn and pointed at me. The worst thing of all was that Alexis was there. She was so scared and I did not know what to do. I just could not believe what was happening.

They raided my house and knew exactly where to find everything since Teri had told them where it all was—including the credit cards that she had stashed at my place without telling me. I was handcuffed and sitting next to my daughter. I had several computers that we used to make the fake IDs, and they took them all. The whole time I was trying to calm Alexis down and all she kept saying was, "Please, don't take my mommy away! Please, don't take my mommy away!"

When they left, I did not even get a citation to go to court. I could not understand the reason, but I was grateful. I was really scared and did not know what was going to happen next, so I called a friend and went to Roseburg for a couple of weeks.

However, my source of income had been taken away and the only way I knew how to get by was dishonestly. After I was caught trying to write an illegal check to a tattoo parlor, I had to come back to Beaverton for a court appearance. I ended up going to jail for two months and thought my world had ended. I was sentenced to stay at a restitution center, so at least I was able to go home at times.

While I was in jail, Alexis' cousin was staying at my house and taking care of her. One day, I came home and they were not there. Instead, I found some paperwork on the table. Angie had forged my signature and was trying to get custody of MY daughter, the only good thing in my life. I also found a letter from my father stating that Angie would be a much better parent to MY daughter than I would. This really hurt me deeply. I just could not believe my own father would do this to me.

I packed up Angie's stuff and kicked her out. Josh came and took care of Alexis the last month of my sentence. Even though he was abusive to me, he had never hurt his daughter, so I knew he would take good care of her and not try to take her away from me. He had always loved her, but his life was no more stable than mine, so he was content to drift in and out of her life.

When I got out of jail, I had to go to a mandatory treatment center. I figured out how to stay "clean" and yet still get high once in a while. I had a similar approach to crime, so I was feeling good about myself. As long as I felt like I was in control, I thought I could get away with anything I wanted to and not have to face the consequences.

REASONS FOR HOPE

In the middle of all this turmoil, I continued to be friends with Cathy and Carrie. I attended church with them a few times and accepted Jesus into my life during an Easter Sunday service. This meant a lot to me, but I kept on using drugs. I continued to have legal problems because of some bogus checks I had written, but my mom paid the attorney's fees and helped me stay out of jail. I was able to graduate from the treatment center and thought I had fooled them all, but in the end I was only fooling myself.

The same day I graduated, I had to go to court again. I thought I would get off because I had successfully completed the treatment program. Then I was indicted. This indictment meant everything would be brought forward, including all the stuff they found when the SWAT team raided my house. My attorney told me that I might have to do some time, but it would be at least two more months before I would have to go to prison.

When I faced the judge for my sentencing, I was a little nervous but took it in stride. After all, this was not the first time I had been in trouble and nothing too bad had happened before. I was convinced this was going to be another slap on the wrist. I would pay some fines and maybe do a couple of months in jail.

"Jamie, you are hereby sentenced to serve 20 months in a women's correctional facility. You have one week to get your affairs in order, and then you are to report to the corrections officer to fulfill your sentence."

I was in complete shock. It was as if it just hit me—what had I done? I was scared to death, not only of what lay ahead, but also because now I had to go home and tell my daughter that I was leaving her, and in only a week. Now, not only did she not have a dad to count on, but she also was going to lose her mommy.

"Alexis, I have to go away for a little bit."

"But why, Mommy?"

"Because I really screwed up, and now I have to pay for it."

"I don't want you to go! Just tell them that you're sorry and you won't do it again. Please, just tell them!"

"I wish I could. I'm sorry, Lex. Please don't hate me. I love you so much. I didn't mean for this to happen."

Those seven days were the worst days of my life, counting down the hours before I would be separated from my daughter, but my family showed their support. I had very little time to make the arrangements for Alexis, but my sister agreed to take her, and I thought this would be the best place for her while I was gone.

My mom had paid for my attorney, but our relationship was strained. I think she got mad because she thought I was going to get off but I didn't. More surprisingly, my dad came to show his support the day before I went to prison. He told me he loved me and that I would always be his daughter. He also said he would come and see me, but he moved to Montana shortly after that and never did get back for a visit.

When my week was up, I was sent to Coffee Creek Correctional Facility to serve my time. The first month in prison is spent in maximum security, no matter what the crime, so during this time, I could not have any visitors—not even Alexis. I was bitter and angry against Teri for taking my daughter away from me. Instead of admitting responsibility for what had happened to me, it was easier to blame it all on her. I eventually realized that I had put myself in this position, and that Teri just helped me get caught.

After I was moved to minimum security a month later, Alexis could apply and get authorization for visitation. At last, I got to see my beautiful daughter, but it was both wonderful and difficult at the same time. All I wanted was to be at home with her. My sister and I also seemed to be getting along well, so I felt like Alexis was in good hands and things would be okay when I got out. I was only able to see my daughter once in a while after the first visit. Carrie helped out by bringing Alexis to a festival at the prison. We were able to spend the whole day together doing crafts and playing games. It was great.

Then I had to go to court again because of some fees and fines that I owed. On the way there, I started to pray. "God, I know that I deserve whatever I get today, but please be there with me and help me through this."

Hope For A New Identity

I know God heard my prayer that day. Mercifully, the judge ended up taking me off probation and dropping all the fees. Because of this break, I would have a better chance to get back on my feet again and make things right for my daughter when I got out.

When I returned to prison, I had to go to medium security to be processed before returning to minimum security. As soon as I had phone privileges, the first thing I did was call my sister to let her know what had happened at court. I was feeling very happy because there seemed to be a light at the end of the tunnel, and I wanted to share it with her. However, her response was not what I expected.

"It's just not working out, Jamie."

"What do you mean?"

"Alexis just isn't happy here."

"Well, what do you expect me to do?"

"I don't know. Figure something out."

I had no idea what to do. I thought that maybe, with a little time, things would get better. But they didn't. When I called back a couple of days later to see how things were going, my brother-in-law answered the phone and started yelling at me.

"Alexis isn't happy and this is putting too much strain on my wife! This isn't working! She needs to go!"

The situation had only created further tension between my sister and me. She had lost a daughter herself and here I was in prison, yet I had a beautiful little girl. She could not accept this injustice and her anger was directed at me.

What was I supposed to do now? I was in prison and could not help my little girl. The only person I could think of to call for guidance was Carrie. I did not know where else I could turn. I never expected her response.

"Okay, let's do this. I love Alexis and God's not going to give me more than I can handle, Jamie. I'll take care of Alexis for you."

I just could not believe what I was hearing. Without a second thought, this woman, my neighbor—not a family member, but a neighbor—was agreeing to take my daughter in. Where did this woman come from? Are there really people like that out there? Now I know there are.

There was another friend who helped support me through this rough time of finding a place for Alexis and dealing with my sister. While I was in medium security, I had met another wonderful woman who loved God with every fiber of her being. She had been to prison several times and this last time, came close to death before being incarcerated. Through her friendship and example I finally started going to church services because I wanted to, not just as a way to spend time with my friends. My relationship with God became personal and important to me and I started going to a daily Bible study.

In Bible study, we were going through the book of

Hope For A New Identity

Acts and talked a lot about the laying on of hands to bring the Holy Spirit into your life. The ladies in my Bible study took me out into the yard, laid hands on me and asked, in Jesus' name, that I be filled with the Holy Spirit. It was wonderful. It was like nothing I had ever experienced. I found that all these women, who loved God, had come to love me. They did not really know me, but it was the love they had in their hearts from God that allowed them to love and help me.

After two weeks in medium security, I went back to minimum for the rest of my sentence. At this time, I had been in prison a total of about four months and thought I only had about nine months left (although I had been sentenced to twenty months, when I arrived at the prison it was reduced to thirteen months). I now found out they later added on the other seven months and I was back up to twenty months. Now, I had to tell Carrie that I was going to be gone longer than either one of us had expected. Once again, I was stunned by her response.

"Okay, God is not going to give me more than I can handle. You need to quit worrying about it. There is nothing you can do about it. We'll just get through this."

Carrie brought Alexis to see me every weekend. I never knew anybody could be like her. She has done and continues to do so much for me. Now I know the meaning of a true friend and unconditional love.

I continued to go to church twice a week and attend

Bible study daily. I was really seeking the Lord whenever I could. I knew that everyone at Carrie's church, Christ Community Church, was pulling for me. The other women in prison knew I was a believer and they left me alone. I also met some amazing women who have gone through the same thing that I have and are mentors to women in prison. I still talk to my mentor and we are able to do things together. It is amazing how many people there are out there that love God and are sharing Him with the women in prison.

While in prison, I decided to try something new and applied to the electrician program. I got the job and it opened doors and my eyes to new opportunity. I started writing to the Oregon Trade Women and IBEW electrical program to try to put a plan in place. When I was released from prison, I started taking a class with the Oregon Trade Women for pre-apprenticeship. While I was there, they paid the $550 fine on my driver's license so I could get it back. I was accepted into the program for pre-apprentice in sheet metal. After several months, I passed the test and I finally made an honest career for myself as an apprentice sheet metal worker.

The Lord has really blessed me. He took care of my daughter while I was in prison and has pulled me through a lot of pain and anguish. I no longer have the anger and stress that I used to have over every little thing.

He has also brought healing to my relationships as

my father and I finally got a chance to talk. I was able to apologize to him and my step mom for everything I had done. I think they could see the changes in my life and knew that I was truly sorry. We had a good cry, lots of hugs and they told me that they never stopped loving me.

The best thing is that now I really know what it means to love. I never was able to love before, not even Alexis. I would get so angry that I would just yell. I did not know there was any other way to express myself. Now I am able to stop myself and communicate in a more loving and caring manner. For instance, this Christmas, when I was not able to buy things for Alexis, I was able to sit down and talk to her about it.

"I'm sorry, sweetheart, I'm not going to be able to do much for Christmas this year, but I'm home."

"That's all I want. Your gift to me is that you love me."

I finally have the peace and happiness I was looking for. I have a future. I do not know what is going to happen tomorrow, but I do know I am going to go somewhere. I have God in my life and I know He loves me.

I am free of drugs, free of crime, free of anger and hate.

I AM FREE!!!

4

HOPE FOR AN ALCOHOLIC

Ron

A jarring collision catapulted me from my seat, where only milliseconds before I had been comfortably at the controls of a digger derrick gouging out a hole for a telephone pole. A full-sized Cadillac had careened out of control, tearing through the heavy gauge metal of my utility truck, flinging my limp body into a mass of churning metal. Mercifully, I was unconscious as I was yanked forward and became wrapped around the axle of the Cadillac. In the process, I broke my back in three places and fractured my arm in several locations, while my femur snapped in two and ripped through the flesh in front of my knee.

The car had struck with such velocity that, after the impact, it spun wildly on the asphalt, spraying a shower of sparks and blood like a gigantic piece of spent shrapnel. I was discovered underneath the contorted mass of metal, an unrecognizable human form.

I regained consciousness in the hospital four days later. By all accounts, I should not have been alive. I was in such agonizing pain that I prayed to die. Over the many months of surgery, rehabilitation and convalescence that followed there was time for reflection. For the first time, I took a serious look at my life.

My father was a successful housing contractor, and I was raised an only child in what must have appeared an ideal family of comfortable means in Lowell, Massachusetts.

For my first four years of schooling, I went to a Catholic Academy run by nuns in Tyngsboro, Mass. In the fifth grade, I moved to a Catholic boarding school managed by Jesuit priests in Andover, Mass. Most of my classmates were also boys of privileged circumstances.

When I graduated from the eighth grade, the son of the Governor of the state of Massachusetts was salutatorian. I was valedictorian. My mother could not stop bragging to all her friends that, out of a class of 150, I was number one. She was particularly excited that I had beaten out the Governor's son for the honor.

My mother, Pauline, was a self-appointed socialite. Among other pursuits, she had hosted several fundraising events for John F. Kennedy during his rookie years in state politics. As a result, he became a family friend, even attending my first communion ceremony. I have a picture of me on this notable occasion, dressed in a little white suit with J.F.K. standing proudly behind me, brandishing that patented Kennedy full-toothed grin. His parental hands are placed firmly on my shoulders. In-

HOPE FOR AN ALCOHOLIC

scribed on the picture in his own handwriting are the words: *"To My Vivacious Pauline: My Most Sincere Love, Jack."* I was only seven years old at the time. I did not know who the man was, but my mother sure did. She was forever forging connections in high places.

Mom skillfully manipulated her influence on my behalf at the boarding school as well. Intermittently, she would drive up like a party girl in her new Cadillac convertible to spread gifts among the priests—a box of cigars for this one, a bottle of fine wine for that one, a special sub sandwich for another, a bottle of whisky here, a carton of cigarettes there. She knew the tastes of most of the priests and catered to them. Not surprisingly, they often winked at my transgressions. It was here that I learned the only thing you can do wrong is get caught. If you get caught the best thing you can do is be well connected and I was.

I escaped harsh punishment during my entire stay there. Others were not so lucky. Vividly, I remember watching three grown men, Catholic Brothers, beat a boy with their fists for wetting the bed. I did not respect the priests. I feared them. As they patrolled the halls of that heartless boarding school looking for opportunities to dispatch the rod of punishment, I saw vengeance and wrath in their eyes—never the countenance of God's love.

My good grades also kept me in the good graces of the priests. An immediate incentive to excel academically was that each month on the honor roll was worth a trip into town to see a movie. I never missed one of those precious outings. None of my scholastic endeavors were motivated by a thirst for knowledge. To me, this was a game of power and privilege. I was in it for present rewards.

Appearances were important to my mother. Loyalty to my father was not. During my stay in the boarding school, my mother began seeing another man. My mother eventually moved to California with her boyfriend, while I stayed in Massachusetts. I tried to numb myself against the feelings of abandonment. I hated the new man in her life.

My dad was my only family contact from that point onward. I looked forward to his visits, but he never had much to say. One time my father visited me mid-week at summer camp. I was lonely for his company, but I could not bring myself to ask him to stay longer. He had taught me to keep my emotions to myself and not to cry, but I cried myself to sleep after he left. I had a father, but I did not have a father's love. The absence of that love was a gnawing pain in my soul.

I spent six weeks a year with my dad, but even during these golden opportunities he kept his distance and I learned to keep mine. I was thirteen years old when he dropped me off at the boarding school at the beginning of the eighth grade. Later that day, he had a fatal stroke. I was sad, but not particularly distraught. I never really knew the man. It was like attending the funeral of a stranger.

About this time, I had my first drink of liquor at a wedding reception. A lady I referred to as my "aunt" would give me her drink to hold while she took a twirl on the dance floor. I finished it and she went to the bar to get a fresh drink afterwards. When she left to boogie again, she would once more give me her drink to hold. This process was repeated throughout the evening. As I downed one drink after another, the liquor took effect, and I loved it. As the warmth of inebriation engulfed me, I felt at ease. I became free from the fear, rejection and sense of abandonment. My anxiousness and loneliness fled. This would be my new friend—the father I never knew. After this discovery, I got drunk whenever I could.

When I moved to Culver City, California to be with my mother and to start the ninth grade, I got on the plane drunk. Soon I was enrolled in a public school for the first time. Also for the first time, my classes were co-educational. I was surrounded by girls. As the "new kid", I captured their attention and started chasing skirts.

For a while I continued to get good grades without studying, but I could soon see that it was not academics that were held in high esteem at that school. It was athletics. By then I was fully-grown and wearing a size 10 shoe, the same as I do today. As a freshman, I made the varsity football team as a fullback. This added to my popularity. My drinking seemed to open doors for me as well. I even conned some of my teachers into being drinking buddies. Between sports, partying and drinking, I graduated with barely a C average.

After high school, I took enough college courses to qualify me for the SAC (Strategic Air Command), but I flunked the EKG part of the physical. I had sustained a brain concussion from playing football. This, complicated by years of heavy drinking, no doubt disqualified me. I was crestfallen. My dream of having a career as an airline pilot was gone.

Perceiving myself as ten-feet-tall and bulletproof, I quickly shook off the disappointment and got a job with the power company as a lineman. Soon I was climbing 90-foot power poles. At first I was scared to death, but I did not let anyone know it. Above all things, I was too proud to admit to fear of anything. I was an expert at hiding my emotions.

For thirty-six years I was a good lineman, but a lousy employee. I worked for a variety of companies in forty-two states. "Take this job and shove it," was my favorite expression. At the slightest provocation, I would walk off the job. I was always savvy enough, however, to have another one waiting in the wings.

Before I would quit a job, I would typically take my telephone test set, climb a pole, tap into somebody's phone line and call around until I found another place to

HOPE FOR AN ALCOHOLIC

work. I was rarely unemployed because I was good at what I did and could talk my way into almost any opportunity. I made sure I had connections.

Ever into appearances, I married a beautiful woman for status in 1965. I was also into womanizing. Because of this my beautiful wife left me. "Big deal," I mused. I knew I was hot property and could have any woman I wanted. I soon found another wife in 1969. She endured seven years of my drinking and philandering before bailing out of the relationship.

My method of drinking was to quickly pour down hefty volumes of high-test liquor until I blacked out. I loved the feeling of letting my subconscious take over while alcohol dissolved my conscious inhibitions and fears. I referred to it as "blacking out," but in reality, I was totally free to let my uninhibited subconscious self take charge. I could expertly carry on a conversation or climb a telephone pole or drive a car and, later, not remember any of it. It was my secret way of coping with life.

Unless people got close enough to smell my breath, most would not even know I was drunk. Faking sobriety was a breeze. Just as I had been adept at pulling top grades and being valedictorian if it pleased me, I could be charming, urbane and an exemplary employee if required. I had learned from the best.

I was the center of my universe, but I would not have

wanted me for a friend. People were for using. It was all about me. I had no loyalty. I was irresponsible and uncaring. I was also desperately lonely, which led to depression. I learned to con psychologists into giving me a mental disability if I needed a break. Alcohol was by then my only friend.

In 1977, I came out to Gresham, Oregon to visit my mother. I was broke and needed work, so I got a job with a local contractor on the "Miracle Mile" in Lincoln City, Oregon. On the final day of the job, I was operating the controls of a digger derrick on the right rear of the truck next to traffic. A few cones had been put out to divert cars and I was raising the boom when a woman in a '72 Cadillac sideswiped the truck with such force it blew out the duals and broke the rear truck axle in two. Inexplicably, I ended up in the wheel well of her car. When the dust settled, the Cadillac was resting 80 feet from the truck with my head wedged under the frame.

It required a tow truck to lift the car off me so that I could be scooped into an ambulance. That alone should have killed me. My body was a contortion of broken bones. My back was broken in three places. My elbow was torn up like you'd rip apart a chicken leg. My shoulder was in the same condition. My right foot was at my right hip and my right femur went out the back of my knee. They never did find my kneecap. My head was flat on one side from being dragged on the ground.

HOPE FOR AN ALCOHOLIC

I was unconscious for four days and in the Intensive Care Unit for forty-two days. Confined to a body cast for five months, I was a hospital in-patient for a full fourteen months. The only good news was that bills were all paid by the State Workmen's Compensation Fund.

No one gave me much of a chance for survival. In retrospect, only God could have seen me through this. If ever there was a time when I should have been grateful to God, this was it. But if I had believed in God, I would have cursed Him for keeping me alive. I was powerless and in pain. My swagger was gone. I could not cheat my way out of this one.

The doctor said I would always be crippled, but I fooled them all. I worked my way back to full capacity. This horrific accident should have killed me, or at least humbled me. It did neither. Eventually, my swagger returned.

Because of the danger of an adverse reaction to my pain medication, drinking alcohol was forbidden during my convalescence. It was the first time I had been sober in years. There was one girlfriend who continued to visit me during this traumatic experience. When I got out of the hospital, we married, but the marriage lasted less than a year. So did my sobriety.

I met my fourth wife, Bev, at a heavy equipment school. I went through this type of training just to keep the government rehabilitation payments coming. Convincing her to become a lineman and join me as a work partner, we completed school together. I wanted to get back to climbing poles again.

However, even in the midst of this new relationship, I found myself being drawn into an uncontrollable sexual addiction. The self-absorbed lifestyle I had lived was doing its work on my mind. I found myself obsessed with women as sex objects. Unable to love, I was driven by an insatiable lust for sexual activity.

My drinking was out of control. I loathed myself and hated my life. Alcohol did not help. It was no longer my friend. I attended Alcoholics Anonymous meetings with minimal success. The more I drank, the more I was drawn to suicide.

I plotted an accident with my boat. I would tie myself up in rope then set the engine at full speed. In the process, I would fall overboard, sink and drown. It would look like I got tangled up in rope—an accident. All of my careful planning was for naught. When it came right down to it, I could not go through with this scheme.

Instead, I devised a plan to take my life by asphyxiation. I connected two large shop vacuum hoses to the exhaust pipes of my '78 Suburban and taped them into the cab. I made sure all of the connections were airtight and the doors were firmly shut, while I climbed into the backseat and went to sleep with the engine running. I woke up with a horrible headache, but I was alive. I was a failure

Hope For An Alcoholic

at both living and dying.

Finally, I admitted to Bev that all of this abnormal behavior was rooted in my lust for other women. That ended my fourth marriage. We divorced in 1998 after eighteen years together.

I moved out of the house, but soon I lost my driver's license because of a drunken driving conviction. I resorted to riding bicycles and started to become physically fit, but my emotional state became worse. My womanizing had taken the shape of hiring prostitutes. I was tired of dating women just to try and seduce them. Why not simply pay for sex? If it was self-gratification I was looking for, why complicate things with trying to establish a relationship? For a short while, this worked.

My brief moments of physical pleasure soon became overshadowed with feelings of emptiness and loneliness. I was getting the physical intimacy I wanted, but I felt morally bankrupt. Was there any hope for happiness? Could there be any peace in my anxious, desperate life?

Then one day, I saw Jeanne. She was walking down the street struggling with some packages. She sat briefly at a bus stop, and I asked if I could help her. She told me she was living at a place called Shepherd's Door, a home for battered women. I knew there must be some story behind all of this, but it did not matter. I sensed my life had begun at that moment. Inexplicably, just looking at her stirred some shred of decency within me. I wanted to help her, not use her. I felt no lust for her, only love. I had regained my driver's license, and I was now driving again. I offered to take her home, and she accepted, but she made me stop a block away from where she was staying. One of the conditions for living at Shepherd's Door, she explained, was that she could have no contact with men. I could not be seen with her. I gave her my phone number and encouraged her to call me.

I thought she liked me too, but a month went by with no call from her. I would rush home from work to listen to my messages, hoping to hear her voice, but, as far as I could tell, she never tried to contact me. She was on my mind constantly, but not in lustful thoughts. I yearned to get to know her just to be friends with her, and, oddly, to serve her. This was alien to anything I had ever felt before.

Finally, I gave up my hope of hearing from her. I had even left a note at her place of residence, to no avail. I pushed this promising encounter out of my mind and went on with my wretched life. Then one day, I came home to hear six messages from Jeanne on my answering machine. Apparently someone had seen us together, reported it and she had lost phone privileges for a month. She was not given the note I left her either. Now she was leaving the shelter, and needed somewhere to stay while she found a new place.

I quickly fetched her and brought her into my apartment. Before she even sat down, she told me that she was a Christian woman and would not engage in sex outside of marriage. It was against my nature, but I honored her request. As our friendship blossomed, we eventually grew more intimate and made plans for marriage. I found a non-denominational minister to marry us in our apartment. In the meantime, my mother died. With the inheritance I received, we were able to buy a home in Aloha, Oregon. The first thing Jeanne wanted to do was find a church to attend.

At that time my job consisted of driving a van to pick up handicapped people. I had recently delivered someone to Christ Community Church in nearby Beaverton, so I blindly recommended it to my new bride. The next Sunday, I dropped Jeanne off there. Eventually, I began attending with her.

I started rethinking my own thoughts on religion. Alcoholics Anonymous spoke of a higher power. I could agree with that, but in no way could I conceive of a personal relationship with God. That was for fools and I was nobody's fool. I had no respect for church. To me, it was a place where weak people went to huddle together in fear of the unknown and made up stories to encourage each other. In addition to witnessing the hypocrisy of the church of my childhood, I had dated a girl from another church where the minister had absconded with the church's building fund. I did not see God in any of that ridiculous behavior.

Jesus was a wishful concept, but not a real person to me. My only emotion toward God was fear. This gave me justification for excluding Him from my life. Who wants to confront a vengeful God? I preferred living by my wits. Over time, however, I was finally starting to be honest about how futile this effort had actually been in my life.

After a few weeks of attending services, the church invited a guest speaker who really broke through my shell of resistance. The subject was a five-part series on the subject of "Confidence." I cannot remember exactly what the speaker said, but by the second message, I was thinking of all the other people whose lives I had destroyed and how selfish I had been. My heart was gripped with remorse and I became ashamed and repentant. For the first time, I felt like a sinner in need of forgiveness. In my heart I was convicted, and I knew that I was unworthy; I deserved God's judgment, not His mercy.

But from somewhere deeper, it was as though Jesus was saying to me, "Come home, my son." Nothing could have sounded more appealing. I had never had a home. I had longed to find a real home my entire life, but I did not know where to start looking.

When the altar call was given, I went forward and, with tears of repentance streaming down my face, I asked Jesus to forgive me. On March 15, 2004, I asked Jesus to

Hope For An Alcoholic

become my Savior and I knew that God had accepted me as His child. Immediately, the self-hatred was gone. The gentle, tender person of Jesus became real to me. The warmth of His love and kindness engulfed me. I had a new friend, a true friend, and there would be no hangover the next day.

It was the greatest day of my life! All these years, I had feared God and never knew I could stand before Him forgiven. By His power, I now have the privilege of being His son. That night was the first time that I ever felt true peace; I was home at last!

Jeanne was ecstatic about my decision. I felt like a gigantic weight had been lifted from my shoulders. Joy was in our home, but I had much to learn about my new life in Christ.

I rationalized that I could continue to drink wine. Jesus turned water into wine, didn't he? After all, I just liked the taste of it. It was not the effect of the alcohol I was going after, I reasoned. Soon I started getting drunk again and even went to work drunk. I could not see it, but I was also withdrawing from Jeanne and becoming my old, abusive self. I had stopped drinking hard liquor, but I soon found wine could be just as damaging.

I had a talk with my pastor and he led me into a deeper walk with Jesus through the power of the Holy Spirit. My wife, Jeanne, had received the gift of tongues, and I was open to any spiritual gifts God had for me.

Reasons for Hope

When I became baptized in the Holy Spirit and began praying in tongues myself, a greater power to serve my Lord was birthed within me. I discovered that I did not need alcohol when I was filled with God's Spirit. Instead of being a slave to alcohol, I found freedom and intimate fellowship with Jesus.

Everyday I spend time reading the Bible. Then, as my pastor taught me, I ask God to speak to me. I often write down the thoughts that He brings to my heart and receive guidance and understanding about my life. The Bible has become a living book. I know God hears my prayers because every day new miracles happen.

Though I had craved and abused alcohol most of my life, miraculously, it now has no control over me. The drinking stopped immediately with no ill effects. There were no cravings, no sweats and none of the hallucinations or delirium tremens that I had experienced when I tried to quit before. This had to be God.

Unfortunately, I had lost my job due to drinking and discovered that no one would hire me. I began to feel more desperate with no money coming in and no medical coverage. My new Christian friends began to pray with me for a job. From nowhere, the manager of a tow truck company took a chance on me. The hours were horrendous and the job was challenging, but, for once, I persevered. I just took one day at a time and asked God to let me help people. My entire viewpoint changed. It was no

Hope For An Alcoholic

longer all about my convenience. Previously, I would have walked off the job without regard to the consequences.

I desperately wanted different employment, but God gave me patience to trust Him to open another door. It was not easy, but I stayed the course. Within a couple of months, another company needed a truck driver who could operate a large crane. This was my cup of tea, but it was a long shot. Imagine my excitement when the Christian manager called to say he wanted me. My pay increased by 40% and included medical coverage. I love the job and the people I work with. What an answer to prayer!

Looking at my life today, I find it difficult to relate to the "old" Ron LaJoie. His world was dark and threatening, filled with selfishness and aggression, driven by loneliness and fear. Today, my world is filled with light. I have confidence, peace and hope. Nothing can conquer me because I know Christ lives in me. I seek only what He has planned for my life. I know it will be good. By His power, I am now a child of privilege.

5

Hope For Overcoming Compulsive Anger

Paul

Y ou son of a @#$%&! What the &*@# do you think you're doing?"

I kicked as hard as I could.

"You #$&%$@* piece of %$#@! Good for nothing, stupid *&#@%#$!"

I got no reaction, no apology, nothing. No response at all. Just silence.

Well, what did I really expect? It was just a wheel, after all. But that did not stop me from getting mad as a hornet at it.

The offending piece of rubber and metal had been attached to the go-cart I was building in the back yard. I was only 12, and I was very excited that I had finally gotten the thing to move. I drove it as far as the front yard before the front wheel fell off, and that is when all hell broke loose.

You do not want to be an inanimate object and get in the way of Paul Botsford.

Of course, the fact that the wheel had fallen off could not be my fault, or at least in that moment, I did not have the logic to see it. In fact, I was not really thinking at all.

The only thing I was aware of was the anger boiling up inside me and I had to release it. When I released, it was like Mt. St. Helens blowing her top.

I kicked. I screamed. I yelled obscenities at the top of my lungs. When the wheel had nothing to say for itself, I flung it out of my sight, as far and as hard as I could.

It took me 20 minutes to find it again.

Later, I found out that my younger brother had witnessed the entire episode from the bathroom window. This was the kind of example I was setting for him: an angry, bitter boy with no self-control. It was just the beginning of a long career of anger.

Looking back, I cannot even say how it all started. I was a good kid, raised in a good home. My parents were still married to each other, I was raised in church and we had a good life. I knew how I was supposed to behave, and I even knew that my angry tirades were wrong. But that did not stop me. In fact, nothing could stop me. When I got angry, it was like something else had taken over, and I had no control over the moment.

I was not proud of my angry fits, and it brought on a lot of soul-searching and guilt. I wanted desperately to get rid of this problem, and I did everything I could think of to get a handle on it. The problem was, I thought I could handle it on my own.

Thankfully, I never got angry with other people, or hit or yelled at anyone the way I exploded at things. In

Hope For Overcoming Compulsive Anger

spite of that, it had a lasting effect on my relationships. I know that I came across as a hypocrite to some people, telling them that I lived by certain standards, but then acting out in completely the opposite way. Yet when I was in the middle of one of my episodes, I could not see that. All I could see was red.

My wife first experienced my problem after we were married. I had become so used to it by then that what was just a minor incident to me, was an eye-opening experience to her and a day that she will never forget.

One afternoon, I was sitting in the living room putting a new set of strings on my guitar. My frustration grew as I struggled with the strings, trying to get them to cooperate with me. I twisted the knob, the string tightened and tightened and the tension grew—and then the thing just snapped. And so did I.

I slammed down the guitar and threw the broken string across the room, all the while cursing up a storm. My wife thought she had married a good Christian man, a quiet, well-mannered professional. That was Dr. Jekyll. For the first time she caught a glimpse of Mr. Hyde.

"Paul, what—?"

But she did not get a chance to ask me what happened because I had already stormed out of the room, leaving my mess behind me. At the time, it did not even occur to me how seeing this side of me might affect her. As usual, I just was not thinking. My frustration mounted, and like that string, I was wound tighter and tighter. I felt like someone else was pulling my strings. I had no choice but to snap.

My angry tirades were not confined to home. If anything, the problem was even bigger at work. After college, I worked as an electrical engineer, designing hardware and software. I worked with test equipment, but it turned out that I was often the one being tested and I usually failed.

Whenever a microchip or a piece of equipment would not work right, I grew more and more tense, more and more frustrated until, finally, I blew my top. I never stopped to take a breath or think through a problem for the clear solution. I would just get angry, and then I would take it out on whatever was within reach. I threw tools, I threw papers, I threw whatever got in my way, and I threw out every obscenity I could think of as I went. This is how my co-workers saw me at that job for almost a decade, as a grown man who threw tantrums.

I felt bad about this side of myself, and I felt guilty that first my wife and then my young children had to live with it, but I also felt completely helpless to do anything about it. So I accepted it and grew accustomed to it, no matter what it did to me.

My breakthrough came when I was almost 32, after we had moved to Colorado. We started attending church and joined a small group that met during the week at

Hope For Overcoming Compulsive Anger

someone's home.

One day, I was having problems with my ear, so I went to the doctor and was diagnosed with an ear infection. When my wife and I went to the home group that evening, there was a prayer time and I asked for them to pray that I would be healed. So everyone gathered around me and started to pray about my ear infection. Well, everyone that is, but my good friend, Dwight.

While we were praying, Dwight had a strong feeling that he should pray about anger. This is not what I had asked for prayer about, so he was not quite sure why this came to mind, and he wasn't entirely comfortable changing the topic of the prayer. But Dwight believed that this insight came from God, so he started to pray.

At first, he prayed very quietly. "God, please release Paul from his anger."

Something happened to me in that moment. I began to have a very physical reaction to Dwight's prayer, like I was wrestling with something inside me. So he became more confident that he was doing the right thing and started to pray louder. "God, please take away this anger that has taken hold of Paul."

Other people picked up on what was happening and they prayed with him. I had asked for them to pray for healing, and even though I had something very different in mind, God knew what I really needed.

The anger that had held me in its grip for so long was

like a bird of prey with its talons sunk deep. That night, I felt the talons loosen and pull away. A burden that had been weighing me down for so many years was lifted, and I left the meeting that night feeling lighter and freer than I ever thought possible.

Not only did I notice the difference in myself, but others noticed it too. It was like I had become a different person, a whole person. I had finally gotten rid of Mr. Hyde and could be one and the same person all the time.

The change became evident to me the first time I ran into a problem at work. It was the same old circumstances, with the same old triggers, but I had a different reaction. The chip I was designing did not behave as I had expected. Normally, I would have started yelling and throwing things. But this time, I realized that I did not have to act that way. For the first time, I felt like I had a choice of how to behave. Instead of just impulsively reacting, I had enough perspective and presence of mind to realize that I could throw a fit or I could control myself, and I made the choice to retain control. It was the most freeing feeling in the world, being free to choose.

But bad habits are hard to break. Over time, I started slipping into my old behaviors. I was afraid of going back to the person I used to be. I hated that person and I never wanted to go back to that place. I talked to a Christian friend about it and shared my fear that all of my progress was slipping away.

Hope For Overcoming Compulsive Anger

"I don't ever want to be that person again, but I'm afraid that I can't stop it from happening."

"Of course you can," he told me. "God has released you from that bondage, and He's given you the freedom to choose how to act. But He can't make that choice for you. Only you can make the choice."

I really took those words to heart. I realized that day that I had to take responsibility for my own actions and take full advantage of the freedom I had been given. Since then, I have been able to make the right choice and walk in that freedom.

Now, when I get frustrated and I feel the anger mount in me, I tell myself, "I don't have to blow up about this. I don't have to be that kind of person anymore."

I thank God that He put someone like Dwight in my life who would listen to Him and have the courage to act on that divine nudging, and I thank God that He released me from the anger that held me prisoner for so long. We all have problems that take hold of us, whether they seem large or small, whether we consider ourselves to be Christian or not, but God can give us freedom from anything that holds us in bondage.

Every day, I rejoice to walk in that freedom.

6

HOPE FOR AN ABUSED WIFE

Audrey

A hammering-like thunder steadily assaulted my ears as I huddled on the couch in the living room, wondering if I should call the police. I could feel the tears beginning to streak my face and I knew my kids must be frightened by all the noise. They probably didn't understand what was happening, but I did not have the words to comfort them. I realized that no amount of wishing could make this go away as the pounding fists continued to rain on the front door.

"Audrey! Audrey, unlock this door right now! Let me in, Audrey!"

If he kept up this racket, I would not have to call the cops—the neighbors would do it for me. But sooner or later, he had to give up. I had to outlast him this time. For once in my life, I had to be strong and take a stand against him.

The wind was knocked from my lungs in shock as the door finally gave way, and I sprang to my feet. There in the doorway stood my inebriated husband, seething with rage. His eyes were crazed, and I could tell by the way his fists were clenched that he was looking for another object to pound. It's not that I feared Richard would harm me. He was not abusive when he was drunk—at least, not physically. The abuse was to my emotions, my self-esteem and to the flickering hope that remained inside of me. He used me, over and over again, and the cycle had to stop. He had promised he would quit drinking. He had asked, yet again, for one more chance. I gave it to him, but he blew it. This time, there could be no more chances.

I pulled my robe tight around me to ward off the cold air blowing in and tried to stand tall. From somewhere deep inside, I mustered what courage I could and found my voice. "Richard, I want you to leave now." I knew he had other places he could go, other women he could stay with. They could have him now. I was through taking him back.

To my surprise, he did not argue but simply turned and left. After a long moment, when I was sure he was not returning, I crossed to the door and shut it. It closed, but the frame was broken. There was no way to lock it. If he returned, I would not be able to keep him out.

With my back against the door, I sunk down to the floor as the strength drained from me and my legs gave way. I let the tears flow freely down my cheeks and hugged my knees tight to my chest. It seemed that my own arms were the only ones wrapped around me.

I had never felt more alone.

Hope For An Abused Wife

"How did I get here?" I wondered. This was not the future I had dreamed for myself. I had grown up in a good family in a small farming community in Nebraska. It was only natural to assume that I would one day marry and have a family of my own. But how did I end up here—a single, working mother of three, huddled up in a fetal position at three in the morning? I just felt so inadequate. Is this all my life would ever be?

I closed my eyes and let the painful memories wash over me, looking for an explanation and maybe for a sign of hope.

After high school, a friend and I had left home for the big city of Omaha to explore urban life. Landing a good job at Mutual of Omaha, I moved into a nearby house with other working girls like myself. My new roommates and I had fun together, spending our weekends dancing and drinking and getting acquainted with young men from the local airbase. I felt like a real adult now, away from the supervision of my parents, and I even learned to look more "sophisticated" by smoking cigarettes (or so we thought at the time). There were no restraints because we were away from home and knew no one in the city who could report back to our families.

One of those weekends, a girlfriend and I had gone to the YMCA for a dance. There were many good-looking men there, but one in particular caught my eye. While I watched him across the room, my breath caught in my throat as his eyes made contact with mine and he crossed the floor to talk to me. He introduced himself as Richard and asked me to dance. I was flattered by his attention and literally swept off my feet by his proficient dancing. It was a night that every girl dreams of and one that I would never forget.

It was not long before I saw him again. I knew Richard was employed as a window washer for the taller buildings around town, and I soon learned that included the one where I worked. It seemed like fate the day he showed up on my floor. I could not avoid watching him; he kept smiling at me as he washed, winning me over with his flirtation. My co-workers could not help but notice either, and I felt proud of the attention.

With that encounter began the relationship that would shape the rest of my life. The attention continued, including regular phone calls and long-stemmed roses when I was sick. This attractive man soon asked me to be his wife, promising me a life of fun and excitement. A little voice inside me expressed reservations, but I ignored it. I was so sure that this was what I wanted.

If only I had known then even half of what I know now. There are so many things I would like to tell that optimistic young woman. But she probably would not have listened to me. This relationship had become a kind of addiction for me. Like an addict, I knew it might be harmful, but I did not want to live without it. I thrived on

Hope For An Abused Wife

the affection, and I would have done anything for love—in fact, I did.

I soon found out that in Nebraska, my fiancé was still officially married to his first wife. But I was too much in love with him to wait for the divorce to become final. So we crossed the state line and were legally wed. It seemed that the life I had always dreamed of could finally begin.

But the dream soon turned into a nightmare. At first, it was just the drinking. I did not see any harm in having a few beers now and then, until I realized they were part of a larger pattern. The drinking made my husband irresponsible with his time, so he had problems holding down a job. Then I found out that the money he made went into his other favorite pursuit: gambling. If that wasn't bad enough, things went from bad to worse when Richard's cousin got out of jail and the two started hanging out together.

But I did not realize just how bad things had gotten until the day the police showed up.

That day I found out that my beloved was a suspect in a robbery. When he heard the police wanted to talk to him, he turned from a suspect into a fugitive. Fleeing the state, he headed for Boston and I, being a devoted wife and not wanting to see my husband imprisoned, supported this decision. Before long, I even joined him. Leaving behind the life I had always known, I packed my bags and moved east.

REASONS FOR HOPE

The day I found out I was pregnant with my first child should have been the happiest day of my life, but my circumstances had become less than ideal. I had gotten a job in Boston, but I would not be able to work with a baby to care for, and I knew I couldn't depend on my husband to be a stable provider for our growing family. I was also very homesick being so far away from the life and people I had always known. Eventually, I was forced to make the decision to return to Nebraska, looking to my parents for help. Although I knew they loved me, turning to them meant admitting my mistakes; it meant facing the reality that my marriage was a disaster. At the age of 23, I had a husband and a baby on the way. I should have been happy. I should have felt fulfilled and loved, but I didn't. An emptiness began to eat away inside of me.

After a time, Richard returned to Nebraska and was fortunate to avoid landing in jail. His return brought me new hope that things were changing for the better. We were back together and no longer in hiding. Our first son was born, and then another. Life was not perfect, but I thought we had finally settled into a stable marriage and at least an appearance of a happy home. It was while I was pregnant with our third child that I suffered the most devastating blow yet.

"You do realize he's been living with another woman, don't you?"

I could not believe the words pouring from my sister-in-law's mouth. Of course I had heard the rumors, but I couldn't possibly believe them. Not my husband. Not the man that I loved, for whom I had already forgiven so much. Not the father of my three children. I refused to believe it.

But it was true. When I confronted him, he did not deny it. We talked about it, and as the tears started to trickle down his face, hope sprang up in my heart. He was sorry for what he had done! He would apologize and we could start over again. But then I looked into his eyes and saw the gut-wrenching truth: he was not sorry for his betrayal—he was only sorry that he had been caught.

The emptiness within me continued to grow. All I had wanted was security and love, but I had been left destitute and rejected. With three children and lacking the means to support my family, my only recourse was to move back home with my parents again.

Then one day, I saw the opportunity for a fresh start.

"Audrey, your brother got a job in Oregon and we're thinking of moving out there, too. What do you think of heading west?"

I was excited at the prospect. In a new place, we could make a new start. There would be new opportunities. Best of all, I could leave my troubles and my past thousands of miles behind me. Like all good pioneers, my parents, my children and I packed our bags and made the journey west, full of the hopes and dreams of the unknown.

Throughout everything, my family was a continual support and encouragement. Where my husband had failed me, my parents helped out by providing us shelter and looking after my children while I worked. It was not how I imagined my life would be as I approached 30, but things finally seemed to be going well for us. I started to believe that things would be okay.

Then Richard showed up.

My wayward husband traveled thousands of miles in search of me, and I could not help but be moved by his plea to take him back. My heart longed for love and I had to believe that I still meant something to him, that he had not forgotten why he had first fallen in love with me. As much as I appreciated my parents, I still wanted a home of my own and I wanted my children to have a father.

So we started over again. Richard promised to attend Alcoholics Anonymous, and I felt like he was finally making a genuine effort to turn things around. I moved out of my parents' house and we got our own home. Richard stopped drinking and we once again started to get our lives in order. We were finally going to give our children the home and family they deserved.

That was until the night that his buddy showed up and they went out drinking again. I just couldn't take it anymore. I had already been through so much and forgiven him too many times. I had given him yet another

Hope For An Abused Wife

chance, but this one had to be the last.

I locked the front door when I went to bed, knowing that Richard had not taken his key. I was not surprised when the pounding started just before three o'clock. But I refused to let him in. He had made his choice and I had made mine. I couldn't live this way anymore.

Thanks to the continuing generosity of my parents, I was able to move my children out of there and into our own house across town. I made it clear to Richard that he would not be joining us. It was the right decision, but a lonely one. The demands of my busy life, as both full-time mother and provider, had limited my social circle to my family and my husband. I knew my parents loved me, but my battered heart still desired the proof that someone outside my immediate family could find worth in me.

Then one day, I made a friend.

Blanche was our new neighbor and a dear woman with a kind heart and open arms. After the death of her husband, she herself also became a single mother, so in that sense she was a kindred spirit. She had a son around the same age as my two boys, so my children also found a new playmate. Blanche welcomed us into the neighborhood and invited us into her home. Yet, as much as I appreciated her friendship, Blanche had an annoying habit: she loved to talk about Jesus.

My family had never been religious, although we went to church on occasion. But I did not need religion in my life, or the judgment of churchgoers as they looked down on my less-than-perfect family. I did not need Jesus and I didn't want to hear about Him. I wasn't even sure that I believed in God—He seemed irrelevant to me.

Even so, I did not shut Blanche out of my life. There was just something about her that drew me to her, and I desperately wanted her friendship. So when she invited us over to her house for dinner one evening, I was eager to accept.

Once we had eaten, Blanche sent the children off to play, allowing the two of us some time alone. She obviously had something on her mind and I had an idea what it was. As usual, she wanted to talk about religion and it made me uncomfortable. But I knew there was something missing from my life, so I opened my heart to listen to what she had to say. Someone had to have the answers, because I knew I certainly did not.

"Audrey, do you have any idea how much God loves you?"

Love. That was the elusive truth I had sought all my life. I knew my parents loved me, but they had never been good at expressing the words. I had reveled in it when I finally found that truth on the lips of a man who wanted me for his own, and I tied my fortunes to that promise. But that promise betrayed me, and my heart had been left void and aching. I wanted so much to be loved unconditionally, faithfully and completely. That is what

HOPE FOR AN ABUSED WIFE

Blanche offered me.

She told me of a God who loved me so much that He would sacrifice His only son for me; a God who loved me so much that He considered me a friend worth dying for. A God who not only accepted me for my shortcomings and failures, but also waited for me with open arms because I was His beloved child, and He would celebrate the day I came home to Him.

Did such a love exist, or was it too good to be true? My soul hungered for it, so when I went home that night, I decided to take a chance. After all, I felt that I had nothing left to lose.

That night in the quiet of my own room, I knelt by my bed in the reverent posture I had learned as a child. Bowing my head and folding my hands, I prayed the only words I knew to pray. But they were straight from my heart.

"God, I don't know if You're real or not, but if You are, please come into my heart and my life."

From that moment on, my life has never been the same.

Something happened in my heart that night. I could feel a change within me and I knew that God was indeed real. With joy, I called my dear friend the next morning and told her what had happened, and she helped guide me in this new journey I had undertaken. She showed me that this step was only the first of many and that I had entered into a new relationship. Like any relationship, it required commitment to make it work.

So my children and I started attending church with Blanche, and I joined a weekly Bible study with her and another friend. After the powerful heart-changing experience of that first prayer, I expected that everything else in my life would change overnight. But it didn't. I became discouraged, as it seemed that my life was still full of worries. What I did not understand yet was that the changes would come over time as I learned to trust in God.

This lesson became real to me one night as I lay in bed, my mind racing with concerns about my job, my children and the many things that occupy one's thoughts in the still of the night. Turning my head to the side of the bed, I expressed my frustration. "Jesus, I thought I didn't need to worry anymore with You living inside me."

The next thing I knew, I was kneeling on the floor. An indescribable presence of love overwhelmed me and my heart was full of joy. I started praising God and thanking Him for these wonderful gifts. Among my many worries, I had been struggling with giving up cigarettes, but the rush I felt at that moment was greater than any nicotine fix. I thought, "Who needs cigarettes? Who needs anything? I have everything I could ever want in Jesus!"

After that night, my life and thoughts were consumed

with God—I never wanted another cigarette. I was eager to share about Jesus with everyone I knew and met. My self-esteem blossomed and I felt I could conquer the world.

I knew my life had truly changed the day my husband came to the door and, once again, asked me to take him back. So many times in the past I had said yes, against my better judgment. My heart had ached for love and was so willing to receive what little he had to offer me. But this time that ache was gone. I had already found a love that was deeper than any I had ever known. I knew that it was unhealthy for my children and me to take Richard back into our home, and for the first time, my better judgment prevailed. I had finally found the strength to say no.

Over the years, I have seen many other blessings in my life, both as a reward for my faith and completely undeserved. Through my relationship with God and my new church community, the emptiness in my heart was filled to overflowing. My Lord and Savior became the lover of my soul and the provider for my family. The bills still came due and the debts still accrued, but I was never in want. When the needs arose they were met, and I learned to give my anxieties to God and accept His peace in their stead.

Moreover, God blessed me not only through His own love, but also through the love of others. At church, I finally found a community for the first time since I had moved to Beaverton. The people I once feared would judge me for my failures instead welcomed me with open arms. More than that, I found that they understood where I was coming from, because many of them had come through the same trials in their own lives. Eventually, one of those friends, a very dear man who identified with my own past, came to love me with the abiding love that I had sought after so eagerly in my youth.

I was 47 by the time I married Charles, and I finally saw my dreams of a happy home come true. God had already given me so much, but through this new relationship, I felt I was given a second chance. I could not erase the mistakes of the past. My youthful decisions had brought much heartache, but they had also given me three wonderful children and a yearning for God. Those choices made me the person I am today—a person who knows a hope and a peace that I might otherwise never have found. But for all that, God gave me the chance to start over again, to finally embark on the relationship I had always wanted.

We were blessed with nearly 25 years of marriage before my Charles went on to heaven. He is there now with our beloved Lord, preparing a place for me when I arrive. But my time on this earth is far from over. God can still use me in the lives of others, the way He used Blanche to help me. Although my parents eventually found the same peace that I did, my children are still searching. So is their father.

I know God can change lives, because He changed mine. I believe He can change the life of my ex-husband. I know that the God who loves me, who sent His son to die for me, is waiting to welcome each of us into His loving arms. He does not care where we have been or what we have done. He is just waiting to celebrate the day we turn to Him and accept His loving embrace. All it takes is a simple prayer of faith.

7

HOPE FOR CHRONIC PAIN

ARLENE

Chronic Generalized Rheumatoid Arthritis. Those were the words that the doctor used to describe the cause of my excruciating pain. But I did not truly understand what they meant until he explained how that diagnosis would impact my life.

"You'll have to stay bedridden for at least a year. This is the only thing that will give your body a chance to stop the damage from progressing." But the doctor's next statement was the one that really crushed me. "Furthermore, you have to stop taking care of your baby. This is putting too much strain on you, and if you want to get better, you must find someone else to take care of him."

Roy, my husband, stayed behind and asked him the question that he was almost afraid to voice. "Doctor, can this condition that Arlene has be fatal?"

The doctor hesitated and then replied, "No, it isn't, but she is going to wish that it were." Roy wisely chose not to share this part of the conversation with me right then.

We slowly left the doctor's office. I had been coping

with physical pain in my body for several months, but this was a new pain, in my heart. I was not going to have my sweet baby, Elden, around to enjoy and care for, and this was a terrible blow to me. Roy tried to comfort me, putting his arm around me as he helped me to the car.

We started for home in complete silence as we let this news soak in and began to ponder what to do. The thought came to me that maybe my mom could care for Elden, and I shared this with Roy. He liked the idea and said, "Well, Elden would only have to be there through the week while I work because Brenda, Dan and I can take care of him and do the chores around the house on the weekends." Brenda, our daughter, was nine years old at the time, and Dan, our son, was eight. I knew this was going to be hard for them at their ages, but it seemed like the only solution.

After dinner that evening, Roy called the children into the living room to explain what the doctor said and how everyone would need to help out. While he talked to them, I phoned Mom and told her the doctor's instructions. Before I even asked her, she offered, "Arlene, why don't you let me take care of Elden for you? You know I would just love to do that, and he really enjoys coming to our house."

Plans were now in place and our new routine soon began. On Monday morning when it was time for Elden to leave for the week, he came into my room to tell me goodbye, holding his little bag of clothes and his well-loved teddy bear. Yes, he was already two and a half years old, but he was still our baby. He bounded up on the bed beside me with a quick kiss on the cheek, and off he went with a loud "Bye." Tears started to roll down my cheeks as I lay in bed and listened to him run out the door.

Alone with my thoughts, I let my mind drift back to how this all started. In October, I had a small attack of the flu that seemed to settle in my ear. The pain did not go away so we visited our family doctor. He could not find anything wrong and suggested we go to an ear, nose and throat specialist.

After poking around on the side of my face, the specialist thought the problem was in my jaw, so he prescribed 15 minutes of rest each hour with a hot water bottle on my face. However, with three energetic children, a husband and a household to take care of, not to mention the upcoming holidays, I did not have time to rest. So I neglected to follow the doctor's orders.

In January, I began to notice my feet swelling—the pain was now in my feet as well as my ear. Our family doctor suggested a neurologist this time, and the neurologist told us to go to an orthodontist. But all these doctor visits were costing us money, and we felt like we were just getting the run around, so we eventually stopped going.

Reasons for Hope

I tried the best I could to get my work done. I would work for a while, and then sit and rest, but it was getting harder and harder to do this and not let my family know how bad I was really feeling. I began to walk with crutches to help me get around.

By February, I could only get around by crawling on my hands and knees because the pain was so unbearable when I walked, even with the use of crutches. The front door was kept unlocked so I would not have to go to the door when someone came. One day, as I was crawling from my room, Roy stopped in at home and discovered me in the hallway. He cried out, "Oh, honey, I didn't know it was that bad for you! Why didn't you tell me?" He quickly came to me with tears in his eyes, scooped me up in his arms, and gently placed me on the bed.

That day, he looked into my eyes and said, "Arlene, you can't go on this way any longer." At Roy's insistence, we drove across town to see Dr. Wolf. The doctor could see the misery I was in as I hobbled over to a chair and tried to sit down. I gave him a history of what I had been through the previous couple of months. He said he had a pretty good idea of what was wrong but wanted me to get a second opinion. Once again, we were sent to another doctor.

Roy helped me into the car and we started through the drizzling rain up Terwilliger Boulevard to see a rheumatologist. I tried to enjoy the scenery overlooking Port-

HOPE FOR CHRONIC PAIN

land as we climbed up the hillside, but something that I used to enjoy looking at did not have the same attraction that day. When we arrived, the doctor took several blood tests and strength-measuring tests, which confirmed Dr. Wolf's diagnosis: Chronic Generalized Rheumatoid Arthritis.

And then the doctor delivered the blow—I would have to remain in bed and give up the care of my family. Along with this, he prescribed medication: Ecotrin (enteric coated aspirin) and Emperim 3. The aspirin was to keep the inflammation in check and the Emperim was to dull the pain. I began taking the Ecotrin right away but decided to hold off on the Emperim for the time being.

This was going to be hard, but I was a strong, Christian lady and I told myself that I could handle it. After all, if it was a Christmas dinner, a house full of company to entertain, or just a well-prepared dinner for my family, I was always up to the task. Since I was accustomed to applying myself whole-heartedly to whatever task laid before me, I expected my recovery to run just as smoothly as my household usually did.

As the weeks progressed, Elden continued to stay with his grandmother throughout the week, while Dan and Brenda looked after themselves and did their homework and chores after school. I could hear the kids moving around the house as they got their afternoon snack, and I so wished that I was out there with them. These were the times when they would share things that had happened in school and we would laugh and talk with each other, and I did not want to miss out on those precious moments. But they always stopped by my room to see me, and I instructed them on the housework that needed to be done. The only problem I heard about was that Dan always closed the drapes in the living room while he folded clothes. As Brenda explained, "He doesn't want anyone outside to see him folding ladies' unmentionables."

Elden seemed to enjoy his weekly outing. There was a tender, sweet moment one Monday morning when he was getting ready to leave. I thought he had already left, and I was crying a little at the thought of him being gone for another week. Suddenly, he came bounding into the room looking for his teddy bear, and his eyes turned to me. He stopped as he saw the tears, came over to my bed and climbed up next to me.

"Mommy, Mommy, don't cry," he said. "You'll get better. I prayed for you, and Jesus will make you better." With that he threw his little arms around me, and I was able to control myself, give him a big kiss and watch him leave the room.

During the daytime, the house was quiet. I had to do daily exercises on my fingers and toes to keep them from bending under and getting deformed. This really hurt, but I knew it was necessary. Roy made a support out of Styrofoam and straps that we put on my feet at night to keep them straight. It was difficult to sleep that way, and so part of my day was spent taking naps to catch up on my rest.

When I was not sleeping, there was nothing for me to do but lie in bed and listen to the cars pass by outside as other people got on with their lives. I felt I needed to keep up my morale for my family's sake, so I found that reading could keep me busy and keep my mind off of myself. Poetry had always been special to me, so I started to memorize my favorite passages. My other main text was the Bible. I began to search diligently through the Word to find out what people did when faced with problems, particularly relating to physical healing. As with the poetry, I occupied my time learning by heart my favorite Scriptures.

I knew when it was about time for Roy to come home each day, so I would begin to sing some of my favorite choruses. This assured him that I was all right, and he would come in and visit with me for a short time.

As our church, Christ Community Church, learned of my condition, they came bearing gifts, especially prepared meals for the family and encouraging words for me. One of my friends suggested that we have a Bible study together, so several ladies started to come to the house once a week. They gathered around my bed, and we would chat about our families, read the Bible and pray. I volunteered to lead the study because I had so much time on my hands, and it felt good to have something like this to do.

I was really enjoying this weekly fellowship until a visit with the doctor determined that I was not healing. "Arlene," he said, "you're taking on too much and it's hindering your progress. Brief visits with your friends are okay, but you need to stop the Bible study. You have to spend more time resting."

I was crushed by this news, but I agreed to stop. I certainly did not want to do anything that would prevent me from healing. The sooner I could get out of bed, the sooner I could get back to my life and regular things like church and Bible studies.

My main company, though, was the pain. While it had started out in my ear, it had by then progressed to a fiery ache throughout my whole body. My feet were swollen and felt like they were on fire. The pain had traveled up to my knees, then to my hips, my rib cage and even the top of my head. It was like having a sprain and then someone hitting that spot with a hammer.

As I lay in bed one day, looking around the room that had become my prison, the phone rang. It was the principal of Dan's school. He courteously asked about my health, but I knew he called with some news about my son. "Dan seems distracted in class. He isn't doing very well in his schoolwork, and his teacher is recommending that he see a counselor. I wanted to let you know so that you can try to get him some help." After thanking the principal, I hung up the phone with a great heaviness in my heart. I could not help but feel guilty that I hadn't noticed my son's problem. He was my responsibility, and I was not caring for him the way he deserved.

When Roy got home, I told him about the call. We agreed to contact Dr. Free, a family counselor, who turned out to be very helpful. He suggested that I move to the couch while the children were home and that Roy take the boys with him whenever he had to work in the evenings or on weekends. He said that Dan was a smart kid but he was not working up to his potential. He was closing in on himself and had told Dr. Free that he was afraid I would not be alive when he came home from school.

I thought to myself, "What is going to happen to us next?"

Between the anguish over my children and the unbearable pain, I decided to finally make use of the Emperim 3. I knew these were strong tablets, but the feeling was beyond what I had imagined. It was like I was floating in air and my mind could not concentrate. Sounds were coming from far off and I began to get sleepy. As the effects of the pill wore off, I decided right then and there that I would not take any more. I did not like that feeling at all, and I told Roy to put them in the medicine cabinet in the bathroom away from me. I would choose the pain over the stupor that was caused by those tablets.

After awhile, people were not coming around as often since they needed to get on with their own lives and responsibilities. It was still winter and each day gave its quota of Oregon rain. My room became darker as the rain clouds gathered, and the sun did not shine for days at a time. The bedroom had always seemed brighter than the rest of the house because of all the windows and the sliding glass door, which was one of the reasons that I had liked it so much. Now, however, the room that I once loved had become like a dungeon to me.

I felt guilty that my children's lives were being disrupted. I had to be waited on by the very ones whom I wanted to help, and I could see that Roy was beginning to grow weary with the extra work and the strain of everything. My condition was not getting better, but possibly worse. I had stopped singing. In fact, I stopped everything that had once encouraged me. Nothing was helping. I was sinking into depression and did not know how to get myself out.

From the depths of my soul, I cried out to God in a very loud voice. "God, see this woman lying here on this bed? She's supposed to be a mother to her three children. She's supposed to be a loving helpmate to her husband. It's not fair for them to be serving me. I should be serving them."

My voice was shaking as I dialed the phone number of my mother. My little boy answered the phone and when he realized who I was, he said, "Hello, Arlene."

This was like a knife stabbing me in the heart.

I told Elden to get his Grandma to talk to me on the phone. "Oh, Mom," I said, "tell Elden that I am his mommy. Please don't call me Arlene around him, and correct him when he says my name instead of 'Mommy.'" At that point, I began to sob. "Mom, I can't stand it anymore. I'm not getting better. I think I'm worse than I was. This isn't working. I will be crippled, twisted in my body, and unable to take care of Roy and the children. I don't know why this is happening to me."

Then I lowered my voice and whispered, "I think I'll take a trip to my medicine cabinet."

There was a silence, then I heard my mom's solemn voice responding. "Arlene, sweetheart, I can't come to get you right now, but I want you to listen to me carefully. You may not completely understand what I am about to tell you, but remember, hell is forever and life is short. If the Lord does not heal you, life is short compared to eternity."

My special mom gave me just what I needed to hear. She did not give me sympathy, as she could have, but spoke truth to my heart. Slowly, I put the phone back on the hook. My tears stopped and my thoughts were twirling around in my head. I knew my mom was in agony and prayer for me.

Suddenly, it hit me. God had heard me. He had answered me in the words that Mom had used to warn me.

I lifted my hands the best I could and said, "Oh, God, forgive me. I'm sorry, Lord, for what I was about to do. Forgive me for doubting You." My words and my focus began to turn to praise the Almighty. "Oh, God, You did hear my prayer. You do care about me." Sweet words of love and praise came spilling out of my mouth and into my soul, like sugar being spooned into bitter coffee.

Suddenly, an awareness of God's presence overwhelmed me. My room became bright with light, just like sunshine pouring out after it has been hidden behind a cloud. Joy and peace flooded my soul. My room changed from a dungeon to a cathedral, and I was laughing and crying all at once with words of praise gushing out to my Lord and God. I was so excited by this that I attempted to jump out of bed. I thought I had been completely healed in that instant. This was not the case, but my healing did begin that day. As I responded to God, my body began to respond to me.

When Roy came in from work, he heard me singing again in the bedroom. As he came to the doorway, he had a smile on his face. He knew something wonderful had happened, and he could see the difference in my countenance. I told him about my day and what had happened.

HOPE FOR CHRONIC PAIN

He rejoiced with me. We called the children in and just spent time together, thanking God for who He is and for each other.

My recovery was a process rather than an immediate healing, but things were different after that day. There remained times of pain and suffering, and the challenge of accepting the necessity of rest. Nothing was going to get me down, however. I knew I could face whatever came into my life.

I began to put into practice a verse that I memorized: "And we know that all things work together for good to those who love God, to those who are the called according to His purpose" (Rom. 8:28, NKJV). I had learned to let go of things. I did not need to drive myself to have everything just perfect, and I learned to take care of myself. I knew the time would come when I could again take on the responsibilities of my family and home—and that time did come.

I rejoiced as Elden began to call me Mommy again. Gradually, I began to stay up for longer periods of time, and by the following summer when we were to visit Roy's family in Georgia, the doctor gave me permission to go. After 18 months in bed, I was finally released to return to society and rebuild a normal life.

This trip was the first time I had been out of the house in months for anything except doctor visits, and it was a true test of how far I had come. Each week brought more strength back into my body so that I could stay up for longer periods of time. By the fourth year of my recovery, I could do most of my cooking, needing just a little help with cleaning and doing the laundry. Everyone in the family had learned to do their part to help me out, so we managed to keep things going quite well. After five years, I was completely healed of the pain that had once permeated my body. I was restored to my family, and I have since been blessed with many years of health and joy. I thank God every day for the miracle He has done in my life and for teaching me how to set aside my pride and self-sufficiency to depend on Him.

8

HOPE FOR A STRUGGLING FAMILY

Jon and Cathy

JON:

That day started like any other. I had worked a long day at my construction job, and I was tired and just wanted to go home and rest. When I pulled into the driveway, I noticed our friends' car. I wondered why they were there. From the moment I walked in the door, I knew something was wrong.

Suddenly, my heart was racing as I found our friend, Patty, holding my three-week-old son—he was not breathing. She quickly explained how she had just stopped by moments before I got there and found my wife passed out in the bedroom and our son, Cody, on the couch turning blue. Instantly, I scooped him up and ran out the door. I was not going to waste any time calling an ambulance.

I jumped into my truck and sped off, heading for the hospital. I turned on the emergency flashers and floored it. With the tires squealing and the motor roaring, I was off like a shot. "Please, God, don't let my son die!" I cried out as I dodged in and out of traffic. I went as fast as I could, not caring about the speed limit. All I knew was that I had to get my little boy to the hospital fast. I could not let Cody die. I jumped up on the shoulder of the off-ramp, roared past all the cars waiting, blew past the stop sign and raced toward the emergency room. Skidding up to the entrance, I jumped out with Cody in my arms. I ran up to the admitting desk and all the commotion quickly got the attention of the nurses and doctors. Immediately, a nurse grabbed Cody and whisked him into a treatment room. In seconds, there were three doctors and three nurses working frantically to save his life. I stood in the corner and sobbed, "Please, Lord, don't let him die…"

CATHY:

I first met Jon during my last year in high school. My older sister was getting married to Jon's older brother, and Jon walked me down the aisle in the wedding. I was just a kid with braces on my teeth, but he was this cool, California dude with lots of confidence and full of fun. He was not interested in me, but we got to know each other a bit when he called our house to talk to his brother. A few years after this, Jon came to visit Ivan and within a few weeks we were dating.

I had grown up in a very close family, raised by my older brothers and sister, all from my mother's first marriage. We were close to Mom, too, but as a single, working mother, trying to make ends meet with a day job as a

Hope For a Struggling Family

realtor and a night job as a motel clerk, all her time was pretty used up. She also lived with chronic pain—the result of a bad car accident that left one leg about two inches shorter than the other. Her back was constantly out of alignment causing terrible headaches, so even when she was home, she seldom had the energy to spend time with us.

As much as I loved my siblings and tried to be like them, I knew that I was different. Mom told me that I came along during her second marriage. The fact that the marriage had failed added to my personal sense of failure, especially since my father had never made contact with me or provided for me in any way.

I never thought about the future or how I could change my situation. I just felt hopeless. But school and my job kept me busy and weekends were for "keggers." I had my ways of coping, so I did not sit around and feel sorry for myself. Why sit around and feel bad when there were so many ways to make myself feel good?

It was not until a couple of years after high school that I learned the truth about the relationship my mother had with my father. I found out from a family friend that my father lived in Portland, Oregon, so I looked him up and called him. In trying to identify him correctly, I said, "Were you married to Joan Fletcher?"

His response stunned me. He said, "Well, we were never married." That was tough to hear. We agreed to meet downtown at a bar. His wife was with him and it was uncomfortable for all of us. We had no further contact after that. I found out that when my mother was first involved with him, she had not known that he was married. When she found out, it was too late; I was already on the way.

When I started dating Jon, we both had an emptiness in our lives, a yearning for something more. There was a need there, but not knowing what we were in need of, both of us felt a relationship was the answer. We both enjoyed partying, so we had a lot of fun together.

JON:

My life had started out with a lot of security. We were living the American Dream, in a new home with a swimming pool in an upper-middle-class neighborhood in Southern California. I was the middle son of three boys. It was the good life: playing baseball, riding mini-bikes and exploring the fields and woods behind our home. But when I was eleven years old, things drastically changed.

Seemingly without warning, my parents divorced and life suddenly became very different. Mom moved my brothers and me away from our new home in El Toro into a rented house in Anaheim. She now had to work full-time to provide for us, and that often left us unsupervised.

The shock of the divorce and the complete lifestyle change left all of us pretty disillusioned. Soon I was run-

HOPE FOR A STRUGGLING FAMILY

ning around with some pretty rough kids. My older brother and I would fight regularly. After one episode where we tore up the house, mom sent us to live with our father in Chicago. After only three months, my older brother moved back to California, but I stayed with dad a bit longer. When I returned to Southern California less than a year later, I found out that I now had a step dad, a step brother and two step sisters. Life continued to be full of turmoil and change.

It was not long before I was running with the wrong crowd. That summer, before junior high school, I got involved with drugs and alcohol. Getting high seemed to take away some of the pain of a life that was often full of conflict and uncertainty. This was to be my pattern for many years to come.

Through all the changes that were taking place, I began to develop a very rebellious attitude. I really rejected all authority. I also felt determined to prove that I could rebel and yet still succeed. I managed to make it through high school, even though partying and getting high were my regular form of entertainment.

After high school, I started making good money as a heavy equipment operator. This enabled me to keep up the payments on my "toys" and also maintain my social life of partying on the weekends. My girlfriend at that time was not the kind of girl any self-respecting mom would want her son to marry.

Reasons for Hope

One day, Mom said, "Why don't you go to Oregon and visit your brother for awhile?"

Work was slow and the relationship with my girlfriend was pretty stressful, so I thought, "Sure, why not." A trip to Oregon seemed like a good change.

After just a few days at my brother's place, Cathy and I started going out. I hung out with her at the restaurant where she worked, and since we both liked to party, it seemed that we were compatible in the most important area of life. We discovered that we were compatible in other ways, too: our lives had been filled with hurt, disappointment and anger from childhood. We both just needed someone.

Within a couple of weeks, I moved in with Cathy and my vacation to Oregon became permanent. Soon, Cathy and I were living at a place in the country as caretakers of a property that her mom was trying to sell for a real estate client. It was a great place to live and I began growing marijuana as a hobby. It was something that I became very good at.

During this time, something interesting happened to Cathy's mom. All of Cathy's life, her mother had experienced severe headaches resulting from a car accident. One of her ankles had been crushed, causing one leg to be shorter than the other. Without corrective shoes on, she could only hobble around the house.

She was a realtor at that time, and through her work,

she met a pastor who invited her to church. He said God could heal her struggling marriage and she should come and have prayer. She had always believed in God and one night she decided to take him up on the invitation. She went to church and they prayed for her.

The next morning she was taking a bath and looked down at her feet and ankles. The skin on her injured leg was bruised black and blue, but there was something else—the fused ankle was normal. The leg that had been two inches shorter now matched the other one and she could walk without pain. The bruising was from the changes in her tendons and muscles, and very soon it was gone. She was totally healed.

This experience set Cathy's mom on fire. She began to tell everyone she saw about Jesus and how she had been healed. She made regular visits to our place and started telling us we needed Jesus, and she encouraged us to go to church. Since we had been living together for quite a while, she also encouraged us to get married—or get divorced. She really just wanted us to either commit to each other or split up.

CATHY:

When mom's life was so changed, it made all of us curious to know more about God, as none of us had ever experienced anything like that. My brothers and sister, as well as Jon and I, began searching for truth like never before.

Jon and I got engaged after four years of living together. We loved each other, but we needed some help with our relationship and we did not know where to turn. The only memory I had of church was when I was about four years old. I enjoyed it, but when someone found out Mom was divorced, they asked her not to come back. She was having a hard enough time being a single mom in the '60s with four children. She chose to quit going. After that, nobody ever told me about God that I remembered, and when I saw what happened to Mom, I was not interested in going to church.

One weekend when mom and I were at the beach, we heard of a group of teens from a church in Beaverton that had come to the coast to make a theatrical presentation of the gospel, and mom wanted me to go. She was still so excited about the Lord and wanted me to experience His love. Soon there was a knock on the door. It was some of those youth inviting us to the play. I felt such emptiness in my heart that I was ready for a change in my life, so I agreed to go.

Watching the play that night, something stirred inside me as I saw and heard the story of how much God loves me. I really needed to know God's love, and I was overwhelmed with a very strong sense that I could be healed of the things that troubled me so much over the years—the loneliness, the shame and the feelings of having been abandoned by my dad. I could get a new start. When I understood that, I just had to respond and ask Jesus to forgive me for all those things that separated me from Him. I wanted it so much. For the first time in my life, I had hope. Right then I prayed and asked God to take over my life. I did not know how totally and completely the power of Jesus could change me. I had so much to deal with and this was my first step. I still had a long way to go.

JON:

When Cathy came home from her weekend at the beach, I saw a change in her. I could tell that her new faith affected her deeply and seemed to really help her, but I was distrustful. I agreed to go to church with her, but since I had never experienced God or had any real religious upbringing, I was skeptical. By this time in my life, I had my own business and was reasonably successful in my new life in Oregon. But there were still many empty places in my soul, and nothing really seemed to satisfy.

After about the fourth church service, I finally let go of the barriers that were holding me back. That Sunday, I realized that I had a big need for forgiveness and that God was reaching out to me in love, rather than judgment, for all the stupid stuff I had done. I asked God to take charge of my life and give me a new start. On that day, the power of Jesus began to melt away the hardness of my heart. I could sense that something really good was beginning to take place in my life.

CATHY:

Beginning in my late teens, I was yearning for some strong figure in my life to help carry the burdens that felt so heavy. I began looking for relationships to fill this place in my heart, though each one just left me emptier than the last. I needed someone who really cared, who would give me emotional support and unconditional love. At last, I thought Jon would be that person.

It was too bad that I had never verbalized this dream to Jon. I had not even verbalized it to myself. It was just an ache in my heart. Neither of us had communicated our emotions to each other. That was a level of intimacy we could not have because we were not able to get "in touch" with ourselves, and that prevented us from dealing with problems that arose between us. We had always numbed ourselves with drugs or alcohol when we felt stress or sadness. It was all we knew—I had started using marijuana as early as the sixth grade.

Once Jon and I were married and trying to live as Christians, we both quit smoking marijuana. But I could not quite let go of the alcohol, and soon the cocaine increased. I could not stop, even though I knew my partying lifestyle was hurting us. I was trying to quit and Jon

Hope For a Struggling Family

was trying to fix me, but it was not working.

We were a couple. We had had a wedding. Friends and family were there. It was great, but it did not really change the tough issues of our relationship. I was still into drugs—freebasing cocaine—and was addicted to a party lifestyle. Jon was not drawn to this anymore and had assumed that when we got married, our old lifestyle was going to change. But it was not so easy for me.

Two years into our marriage, we decided to start a family, but my first three pregnancies ended in miscarriages. I quit my job to try to trim some stress out of our lives, but I was still doing the drugs. I wanted to change so I joined Alcoholics Anonymous. I got some help and I would sometimes go months without using. But something would always happen and start the cycle up again. During these extended periods of being clean and sober, I began to realize that I did not know who I really was. For so many years, I had been stuffing my feelings and numbing the pain every chance I got. It was refreshing to be of sound mind.

One Sunday morning at church, an older couple prayed for us. They knew we wanted a baby and they prayed specifically that God would give us a child. Within a month, I was pregnant.

Nine months later we had a beautiful baby girl. I really loved her, but it was not enough to fulfill me. My addictions were still driving my life. Within 18 months I had another child, a beautiful baby boy.

JON:

It was so crazy to me that, even after we had become Christians, seen miracles of God in our lives and started our family, Cathy stayed connected to friends that were really dragging her down. She was living a double life and it was making me mad. I was eaten up with worry for our children and anger with her for putting them in such danger.

It was not uncommon for me to come home from work and find that she was out partying. One time, I decided to go look for her. I drove around to her usual hangouts, but could not find her. After I had returned home, she came in and she was loaded. I was furious and she knew it.

"Where were you? I went out looking all over for you!" I yelled at her.

"What do you care? I wasn't doing anything," she replied in a sulky voice. We went on exchanging insults and the fight was heating up. "Go ahead, hit me. Hit me!" she dared me. She could really get in my face with her attitude.

I had had enough, so I grabbed her and threw her on the bed. She came back with a smart comment, and I turned around and hit the wall with my fist as hard as I could. I put a hole through the sheetrock on both sides of the wall, not to mention the damage I did to my hand. I was not even thinking; I was just letting my anger drive my actions.

Another time, when Cathy was gone, I knew she was with this guy that had started her on freebasing cocaine. I once had considered him a friend, back when we were all doing drugs, but that friendship was now long gone. I was so mad that I took a shotgun and headed for his house. I was going to "off" this guy for introducing Cathy to another addiction. I made the forty-minute drive to his house, and with each mile the anger just boiled inside me.

When I finally reached the house, I grabbed my shotgun and jumped out of the truck. Cathy's car was not there, but by now there was no stopping me. I headed for the door and started pounding on it. He must have been passed out inside not to have heard me. Thank God he did not open the door, or I would have been looking at a murder charge. There was a huge slab of granite by the front porch, and in my rage, I picked it up and slammed it to the ground. With a loud crash, it broke into pieces. That is what I really wanted to do to him. I was so frustrated and angry that if he had come to the door, I am sure I would have killed him.

The anger took control of my life. I could not think about the situation with Cathy without getting boiling mad. I loved her so, but I felt so hopeless in the endless cycle of drugs and periods of sobriety. I had gone to an attorney and made arrangements for a divorce. We had children that needed a mom. I told her, "Get out! If you want to have that kind of life, I'll take care of the kids myself," and I threw her out of the house.

Our relationship was a wreck. Cathy would come and go as she pleased. Things would heat up and she left. Then they would settle down a little and she came back home.

CATHY:

With the birth of our second child, I developed Postpartum Depression accompanied by severe headaches. I got through some of the depression by taking Prozac for a couple of months, but the headaches persisted and were very intense.

My doctor knew I was having trouble, so he wrote me a prescription for Valium and Somas. Somas were a new muscle relaxant and it was believed they were not addictive. Maybe one was not, but when you take four, you can get high. Whoa, that was just what I needed! I could get 50 at a time. My doctor did not seem worried. He just kept writing the prescriptions.

When Jon realized that I was "hooked," he responded in his usual way: anger and frustration at me and at the doctor. He finally went down to the doctor's office and told them about my past drug history. The doctor asked me, "Is this true?"

Hope For a Struggling Family

I said, "Yes, it is." The doctor assured Jon that he would no longer prescribe any more drugs for me. A few weeks later, I was struggling and called the doctor's office. Another prescription was issued, no questions asked. When Jon found out, he was furious. He called the doctor and threatened a lawsuit, so I was dropped as a patient.

I had seen it coming and I was prepared. I had pills stashed all over the house, and one of my old friends had told me how to get the prescriptions on my own. I then mischievously set out to phone in my own prescriptions. Then, the next day, I went over to the pharmacy and picked it up. It was pretty scary, but kind of a rush, the suspense of whether they would fall for it or not.

I got away with this for some time, but one day when I went to the pharmacy to pick up my prescription, they took longer than usual. I saw the clerk making a phone call, and I began to feel anxious and just had to get out of there. I headed for the car and as I was getting in, the police pulled up. I was charged with forgery and falsifying medical records. I did some jail time and a lot of probation. These were rough times. I never expected to end up in jail. I would say it was a new all-time low in my life, as well as my marriage.

During this whole time, I had been trying to find help. I attended AA for a couple of years and went to a group called Lion Tamers, a Christian version of AA. One night at a meeting, after I had been clean and sober for a few weeks, I had an emotional outburst. This was very different for me. Usually, I was withdrawn and concealed my emotions.

It was at this time that I realized after all these years, I never really knew who I was. I had not allowed myself to walk openly in my feelings, ever, and was never able to express who the real Cathy was. This began some real healing and growth. There were times, though, when the urges were just too strong to resist and I would relapse again. At one point, I saw how it seemed that people would just change their drug of choice, and now it was only the meetings that could keep them clean. It seemed like if they were to miss a meeting, they would relapse. I wanted more than to barely hang on. I wanted total freedom. So I asked the Lord to show me how to get that freedom and quit going to the meetings.

At church, people cared and prayed for us and wanted to help, but they did not know how to deal with the kind of intense needs we had. We went to mom's church down at the coast, where she had been healed, but we could not find the level of healing that we really needed.

One night at the coast, the pastor picked up the phone and called a person he knew whose grown children had worked with a ministry that really helped their marriage. It was called Marriage Ministries International. We managed to get ourselves invited to an "outreach" meeting, which was a graduation for an MMI class, where each couple shared their story.

That was an amazing night. These people had come through some very extreme problems. One woman was a police officer in a small town. She used to beat up her husband, and here they were, acting like a couple of newlyweds. Each couple had a unique and very difficult story, and as they talked, we began to feel like these were people to whom we could relate. After their stories, they would not be shocked by the stuff that was going on in our lives. Maybe there was hope for us after all. We wanted to get involved, so we signed up for a class. We could not wait.

At first, nothing happened. Nobody called. About five months later, I called Al and Patty Cheston, the area directors for MMI, and begged them to help us get started. They did not have any classes starting, but I continued to push. Finally, Patty said they had a leadership-training weekend in Pendleton coming up, which was really for people who had already completed the course and were going to be leaders. I pushed some more and they said we could come.

When I told Jon, he called Al and really grilled him about Marriage Ministries International. He was suspicious and demanding about what they could do for us. He wanted some kind of assurance that this would really help. It was a demonstration of his loss of hope that we could get better, but Al just smiled and said, "I can't guarantee anything. It just depends on what God does."

As it turned out, Jon's company was sending him to Eastern Oregon about that time. We took off for Pendleton with a fifth-wheel trailer. The first weekend we were there was the leadership-training weekend.

JON:

We soon learned that Marriage Ministries International uses the Bible to teach what God planned for a marriage to be. The class we took had homework for each lesson. On the leadership weekend, there is only time to do one of the homework sections.

The homework for the training weekend was on forgiveness, and the Bible reference was Matthew 6:14-15. It said that if you want to be forgiven, you have to forgive others. This presented a major problem for me because my heart was very hard against Cathy. It was as if I had a six-foot wall of stone in my heart from all the years of pain. I had not served the divorce papers yet, but I still had them. I was only tolerating Cathy and she knew it. She tiptoed around me like a little, whipped puppy dog. I was preparing myself emotionally to end the marriage.

I prayed, "You know, God, I'm really stuck here because I've got to forgive. I know how much I need Your forgiveness to cover my many sins, but I feel so justified in my unforgiving attitude toward Cathy. I don't want to

HOPE FOR A STRUGGLING FAMILY

forgive her, but I see that I have to."

I was afraid to trust God. The thought of opening up and trying to love my wife again seemed too risky, but sitting in that fifth-wheel trailer in Pendleton Oregon, I turned to Cathy and said, "I forgive you." In that moment, a small hole was drilled through the stone wall in my heart and a ray of hope began to shine through. It was a small start, and I was very leery of putting too much faith in it, but that little ray of hope was like a sip of water to a man dying of thirst.

CATHY:

I believed that weekend together was a miracle. When Jon told me he forgave me, I felt the same hope that he did. Again, I started badgering Al and Patty to get us into a class. Finally, they said, "Okay, but you have to be the assistant leaders, and it has to be at your house. It's also going to take two nights of your time each week—one for prayer and one for the class." They knew that if it were at our house, we would have to be there. No skipping out midstream.

This began a major change in our lives as we studied the Bible together and prayed, "God, change *me*," not just the other person. It also began a close relationship with Al and Patty. They became like surrogate parents to us. We knew they were fighting for us and for our marriage. In the weeks to come, a lot of ugly stuff was vented in our times together. But they held on to a picture of us as a healed, loving couple and did not give up on us.

JON:

One night when Al and Patty were over, and I was going off about Cathy and all her problems, Al said to me, "What about you, 'O man of God'?"

I just about hit him, I was so mad. How could he take Cathy's side? I was the one that had to put up with all her stuff.

Patty followed it up. She was fearless; she drilled her finger into my chest and told me, "You need to forgive her." They were right, of course, and even though I had forgiven Cathy that day in Pendleton, there were still things that I was holding against her that I was not ready to forgive yet.

CATHY:

As we had our third child, Cody, I was filled with turmoil. How can I be a mother to these children? I had never received much guidance or training in this area, and I was feeling bankrupt as a wife and mother. Jon and I were still having such a huge breakdown in our communication, and it seemed that I was the problem—at least that was Jon's point of view. I was trying hard, but it never seemed good enough.

The children were so close in age that I was always

exhausted, and the drugs made it all so much easier to cope. So I continued to use them, not understanding the extent of the damage I was causing. All I knew was that it was hard to pray and find God's peace alone. With the children, I never had time to spend with other people, so I did not have any close Christian friends to show me the way. Again, I was drawn back to what I had always known: self-medication.

JON:

It all came to a head that night I came home from work to find Patty sitting on the couch holding my lifeless son in her arms while Cathy was passed out from her "prescriptions." Once I reached the emergency room, the doctors swept Cody away and worked on him for about 45 minutes before they got him stabilized. By now, I was nearly in shock. All I could do was wait helplessly and beg God to save my son. I had no idea if he would live or die.

Cody spent the next four weeks in the Intensive Care Unit at Emmanuel Hospital. The doctor was having trouble pinpointing the cause of his trouble. Cathy and I were there with Cody one night, and I was again "going crazy" with Cathy. She needed to understand that she was the cause of all of this. Since we were in a hospital I was trying to be quiet, but I was so angry. "Don't you think I know it's my fault? Do you have to keep telling me?"

Cathy said.

"Well, you don't seem to be getting it, do you? Look what you've done now, Cody could die," I kept telling her. I was going on and on with her, quietly but intensely. Then a nurse came in and overheard me talking about the drugs. Cody had been tested for narcotics, but Cathy was on Somas and they had not tested for that.

The nurse took it from there. Cathy was nursing and Cody was getting drugged through the breast milk, but it was a very heavy dose for his little body. The hospital reported this to the Department of Human Services, and we were looking at the possibility of charges of neglect and having all our children taken into protective custody or foster care.

It was a very dark time, but God proved He was there for us in different ways. A good friend of mine invited me to go to a meeting of the Full Gospel Business Men one night. He knew about Cody being in intensive care and that I had been spending all my time there with him, so he thought I could use a break. I could not bring myself to leave, but I asked him to pray for us. That night someone passed the word to the group, and several hundred people prayed for Cody and for us, even though they did not know us. A man stood up at the meeting and told the group what he felt God had spoken to his heart. He said that Cody was not going to die and that God was with our family. When I heard that, I was really encouraged.

A court hearing was held on the issue of neglect. It was tough to take, as my own kids became the evidence of our dysfunction as a family. I listened to testimony from the hospital staff, from the Department of Human Services and others. Then the judge pointed to me and said, "Why did you let this happen?" He basically put it on me. He said, "If you knew she was having problems and you left her with the children, this is your fault."

That was a wake-up call. I had nothing to say for myself. In my mind, I had drawn up a strong case against Cathy, putting all the blame on her. I was innocent. I was the faithful father that picked up the pieces after she messed up. I was holding down a job and trying to take care of the kids all by myself. When the judge said that to me, I could not deny that I had left my family in jeopardy. We almost lost Cody and I was guilty along with Cathy.

I know now that the Bible speaks of judges as God's instruments, placed in authority over us. It was not my custom to acknowledge and respect authority figures, but when the judge pointed his finger at me, I felt shame—and I knew he was right. The weight of my own guilt now shook my soul. For some time, I was not able to bond with Cody, but I have since realized that one of my greatest problems was the shame and lack of forgiveness I felt toward myself for all that happened to my son. God has given me healing on this and Cody and I have become close, but it sure was a dark time for me.

Things began to settle down a bit. The neglect charges were dropped, and we struggled forward as a couple. Al and Patty continued to come over each week for our MMI class, and we kept working on becoming the couple that God planned for us to be. There were so many layers of healing to work through, and help came from many different sides. God placed a team of people in our life to help us which included that judge, the Full Gospel Business Men's Fellowship, Marriage Ministries International and our home church, Christ Community Church.

CATHY:

The freedom from the drugs that I sought for so long did not arrive with a dramatic healing, but came little by little, while I was doing a Christian Bible study called "Search for Significance" with a friend.

One day, she asked me a question. "What is the name you feel you've been given by the world, by life?" I would have thought it would be "Rejected," but immediately I knew that the name was "Illegitimate." It surprised me to have that word pop up, but it was true. I had always felt illegitimate. Suddenly past conversations on the subject came to mind, and I knew that I had lived my whole life under that label. My friend suggested that I ask God, "What is the name You have given me, Lord?" And I

Hope For a Struggling Family

clearly heard his response: "Precious Daughter."

This thought was quickly followed by another thought, which I believe God gave me. He said, "Your name is changed to 'My Beloved Child.'" That was a healing moment. The acceptance I had been longing for my whole life had now come. What God thought about me sunk deeply into my heart and changed my life. I never used drugs again.

I did not say much to Jon about it, but three days later he came home and said, "*You* are a different person."

People have asked me why this did not happen sooner. Maybe it could have, but I doubt that I would have heard it. I had so much baggage. God will do only what we let Him do at any given time. When we maintain control of our life through wrong patterns of thinking and acting, our progress is slowed. When I came to God, all I knew was wrong patterns, but He brought healing and changes into my life, one layer at a time.

When we search for God's deliverance with our whole heart, He sets boundaries—we are living proof of that. We were not destroyed as individuals or as a family. We have had healing for so many things, and we have broken a pattern of dysfunction for our own children that had gone on for generations. They will live their lives free from so much of what hurt us, and they can stand on our shoulders and move ahead with strength. Our older ones lived through some of these hard times with us, and we have gone through some healing with them because of its effect on their lives. Today they are strong young people.

We are all still in the process of God's changes. That's the way it is with most people I know who are in church. The church is definitely a hospital for the hurting, not just a place for saints. I do not have the same hurts I had a year ago. I receive more healing and more "life" as I learn to depend on God's strength, and He is faithful.

Through it all, and after more than 23 years together, we can each joyfully say that there is no one else that we would rather be with! God is so good!

9

HOPE AFTER DESPAIR

Sri

My grandfather was a Hindu priest for the Devanga Caste in my home city of Dodballapur, India. He was a very responsible man and served the community well. He performed marriages, the blessing of homes and ceremonies we call Pujas, or rites of devotion to gods. He taught the Hindu religion to his children so, even though he died before I was born, his influence was strong in our family. Within the family, we were expected to perform the rituals and read the scriptures. We had worshipped many gods—one for each creature.

My name is Sridhara Purohith. My last name, Purohith, means "priest" in my native language of Kannada. I am a devoted son. As with many from India, I would never shame my family in any way. The close ties within the family encompass our entire lives and fortunes. We work together and take responsibility for each other in all matters. We trust our parents to arrange a suitable marriage partner for us. They know us better than anyone else and we trust their wisdom to choose for us. They also help us as children are born, often taking most of the care of the young ones while parents are working. At the end of our parents' lives, one of the children becomes the caregiver and is responsible to shelter them lovingly during their older years until they leave this life.

It is amazing how extended families live and work together in India. Yes, some families have a tough time of it, but that is the way it has been with us for a very long time and we are devoted to each other in spite of differences of opinion. These values have held our culture together for centuries.

My father, along with his two brothers, was in the silk business. My father was the middle brother. His job was weaving and helping in other parts of the family business. The traditional way is for all of the children to join the business. This increased work force results in increased productivity. Each individual is important. The business was going well and my uncles wanted to build it further.

My father saw the future of the silk business changing. He sensed that whatever business we were in, without education, the children would always be limited. Eventually, this brought a break with his brothers. To their way of thinking, there was no time for schooling. It was a waste of time and money. They also had a fear of education. They believed that the children would lose respect, parents would lose control and children would

Hope After Despair

leave home. This could be disastrous to the family structure and the traditional family business.

After much deliberation, one day my father said to them, "I want to get an education for my children. If it becomes necessary, I am ready to leave." And that is what happened. My father made a break with his brothers and took steps to see that his six children received the best education possible.

Because of this decision, our family came under many pressures. We felt rejection, shame and persecution from my relatives. We also had increased financial pressures due to losing the income from my father's family business. The cost of education for the children was a burden. In addition, my three sisters were almost grown to marriageable age and there were no prospective bridegrooms coming forward due to our financial situation. Their chances of marriage to someone who would be able to provide for them and love them would not be good.

The pressures were like a dark cloud over us in every area of life. Even in day-to-day things, we were not able to move forward. Fear of the future and hopelessness hung over us. The pressure to excel in school was almost overwhelming. Our ability to study, do well and get a good-paying job was the only hope for our family's financial survival.

I followed in my older brother's footsteps and studied computer engineering at a college in Davangere. Just before graduation, my brother made a job contact for me in northern India near Delhi. I managed to get a job as a software consultant. I was anxious to get started so that I could provide money to help my family. I traveled a lot in my job and, in no time, I realized that the success of landing a job did not alleviate the pressures and fears that I experienced all through school. I felt restless and unequipped to do my work.

One day, on my way to a customer site, I was waiting for a train in Mumbai Central Station. As usual, I was very nervous about my upcoming assignment. To kill time, I was looking around a bookstall. I was scanning the books on the rack and my eyes encountered the phrase on the back of a book that said, "This book can change you." That idea definitely captured my interest. I picked it up and flipped through the pages. I read, "I can do all things through Christ who strengthens me." (Philippians 4:13, from the Bible) I turned a couple more pages. I read, "If God be for us, who can be against us?" (Romans 8:31)

I was not looking for a new religion at that point. My own religion had not brought any answers to the deep concerns and pressures of my life. It was simply a part of our culture—part of our family, but on an individual level, it provided no help to me.

Something happened to me when I read those verses from the Bible. I did not know anything about Christian-

Hope After Despair

ity until then. I knew that there were Christian hospitals and Christian schools, but I was usually not very open to reading books about such things. I knew nothing about Jesus, but the text that caught my eye and commanded my attention was, "I can do all things…" That was a very hopeful phrase I had not heard in my life until then, and I wanted to know more.

I bought the book, *The Power of Positive Thinking*, by Norman Vincent Peale. That book, in a very simple way, teaches about how to pray. Dr. Peale says that if you have any needs to go and talk to somebody at the church. He told a story about a man who came to him with a tremendous need and, after prayer, the person was healed and his prayers were answered. That was a new concept for me. It was a totally foreign idea. I had seen so many financial and physical needs—both my own and that of others. I would go to the temples for comfort, but felt no relationship with a deity. I was not able to ask for help from any god. Even if I asked, I did not know if "He" would give. It was more about my need to become a better person—to make myself better—than receiving help from someone who could deliver me out of my problems.

That book filled my thoughts. It said that if you have any needs, you should go and get prayer at the church. On the way to my office there was a church, but I was always hesitating, feeling strange about asking someone that I did not know to pray for me. As a Hindu, I could see that if someone needed help and asked me about my religion, I would not be able to give them an answer that would help them.

Finally, one day I went into the churchyard and there was a man standing next to a tree. I said to him, "I want to know more about Jesus. I don't know about Him. Can you help me?"

The man said, "There is a person by the name of Sathyaraj at the administrative office at the church. He can help you. Go and meet him."

So the next morning, I went to see Sathyaraj and said, "I want to know more about Jesus. Can you help me?" He took me inside the church and we sat together while he drew a picture of a circle.

He said to me, "This is your life, and you are here in the center, controlling your life. All the fears that are part of you control your actions and your reactions. Your life is controlled by the fears. Today, you can put your faith in Jesus and He will become the center of your life. He will take care of all your fears and all your needs. He will be with you. He will provide you with whatever you need. Are you ready to put your faith in Him?"

A feeling that I was going to be released from the thoughts and fears that plagued me arose within my mind and heart. I was certain I was going to be benefited. I said to him, "I do not understand all that you are telling me, but I want to come out of the life I am living. If praying

HOPE AFTER DESPAIR

to put my faith in Jesus is what I need, then that is what I am going to do."

Sathyaraj led me in the prayer to receive Jesus into my heart. I asked God to forgive the things that separated me from Him, and come into my life and change me. That was one small step. My life was beginning to move forward.

I was only able to spend a very short time with my new friend, Sathyaraj, and I was encouraged by his prayers. Soon after that, I got a new job and moved to the United Kingdom. Sathyaraj encouraged me while I was in the U.K. to look for a church that could help me grow in my faith. "Call the church," he said, "and they will help you out." In the U.K., I had attended a catholic church and was encouraged by the services, but soon I was moving again—to Iraq briefly, escaping just before the first Desert Storm war.

Next, I had a transfer to the U.S. Again, my friend, Sathyaraj, encouraged me, "Call the church—especially an Assembly of God church, and they will help you out."

In February of 1993, I arrived in Oregon. When I came here it was a great feeling. I started to like it right away. Friendships with other young people like me, who were employed by the same India-based company, came easily. We were all far from home and depended on each other as "family." Every weekend we would rent cars and go for trips. Very soon, I became concerned because too much of my income was going towards my lifestyle. My goal had been to send money home. Work also presented a lot of pressure.

One evening I called my friend, Sathyaraj, and he reminded me again to call the church. I was not sure how the churches would treat a foreigner. I did not have any connections, but I decided to do it, to listen to my friend.

In the Yellow Pages, I found Christ Community Church and made the call. A lady answered the phone. I was very encouraged to hear her quiet, soft and kind voice. I had not heard a voice like that before. I told her, "I'm a foreigner here. I came from a Hindu background and would like to know more about Jesus and how I can be helped."

She said, "My name is Sharon. My husband is the Pastor of this church and he will get in touch with you." I can say that a lot of blessings have come into my life, but I cannot forget that call. It was a very significant telephone call in my life.

Right away Pastor Morse called me back. He was so kind and compassionate toward me. I was really encouraged. I felt I was valued and respected as a person and there was a godly presence in his voice. He respected me even though he did not know me, or where I came from. He valued me as a human being.

Since I did not have my own car, the Pastor arranged for me to get a ride to the Sunday service. Saige was very

Hope After Despair

kind and gracious. He was a man with children and a family, but he took the time to pick me up. I did not know what kind of clothing to wear. It was so funny—the first Sunday morning I came with a jacket and the other men were wearing suits. So I said to myself, "OK, this evening I will wear a suit." So that Sunday evening I wore a suit and everybody else came dressed casually.

The first time I was in Sunday School, I remember it was an amazing experience. I could feel God's love and His presence in the people there. People came forward to meet me and were very welcoming. They were sincere, compassionate and interested in me. I had not been sure what I was getting into, but in that church, everybody made me very comfortable. Then we went to the worship service. The worship was very personal. I watched the people and saw the intensity of their worship. I wanted to have that kind of relationship with God in my prayers.

I was beginning to understand. Christianity is more than a philosophy or religion. It is a relationship. At first, I was not comfortable to pray like others. I was not confident to go to God like they did. I did not feel righteous and holy to approach God. My background reminded me that I had not done my part to earn anything from God. Everything was still so new. I did not know where to start.

One day, I told the Pastor of my dilemma and that I had many questions. We agreed to meet for lunch each week. Pastor asked me to bring my questions and we would discuss them. I had a long list of questions and he was happy when he saw them. My first one was, "What is my purpose in life?" Each time we met, we talked more about each one of them. My pastor was very patient and encouraging in answering my questions.

The Holy Spirit was working. It was a power greater than I could comprehend. I was just taking one step at a time. I came to trust the people I was with at the church as I saw the sincerity in their fellowship with God and toward other people. I wanted to become like them. One couple, Roy and Arlene, who were the age of my parents, took an interest in me as if I were their own son. I did not miss my parents in their presence.

I became part of a small group going through the scriptures to learn the foundations of Christian faith. I did not understand everything, but I was taking baby steps. We learned the scriptures:

"And this is the testimony: God has given us eternal life, and this life is in his Son. He who has the Son has life; he who does not have the Son of God does not have life." (1 John 5:11, 12 NIV)

"Until now you have not asked for anything in my name. Ask and you will receive, and your joy will be complete." (John 16:24 NIV)

HOPE AFTER DESPAIR

"No temptation has seized you except what is common to man. And God is faithful; he will not let you be tempted beyond what you can bear. But when you are tempted, he will also provide a way out so that you can stand up under it." (1 Corinthians 10:13 NIV)

"Trust in the LORD with all your heart and lean not on your own understanding;" (Proverbs 3:5 NIV)

"If we confess our sins, he is faithful and just and will forgive us our sins and purify us from all unrighteousness." (1 John 1:9 NIV)

All the scriptures were really speaking to me at the time. My faith began to grow. I began to know that God loves me as I am.

As time passed, I began making preparations to return to India for a visit. I felt I came to church as an orphan and I was returning home as a missionary. I wondered what it would be like to go there as a Christian in my newfound faith.

My family had a lot of expectations of me. They had made great sacrifices for me. Their hopes and dreams depended greatly on whether or not I could come through. Would they reject me? Would they feel that I had rejected them because of my faith in Christ?

I talked to the Pastor about this and he said, "Because

you believe in Jesus, you will be more loving and more caring toward your family members. It is not that you will grow away from them, but that you will become even more responsive to them. Also, the Holy Spirit will go before you and He will be the one to help them see that you are even more of a son. A better son. Don't worry. God is going ahead of you."

That is how it happened. God did open the way and they were very happy about all the things I had accomplished. I had been able to help my family with finances. My parents had found good husbands for my sisters and the family debts were settled. I did not do a lot of talking to them about my faith, but they acknowledged the change in me. I let my life speak.

Soon after that, my family began to look for a match for me. Parents are responsible in this way and they looked for quite some time. They made contact with an elder in my town who was my father's classmate in school. He was an educational officer for the whole of Taluk, which is like a county. My father, brother and elder sister went to meet with the family and with my prospective wife, Vinutha. This was favorable on both sides, so when I came home, they arranged a meeting.

My father, brother and I arrived for our appointment. Vinutha and I visited together and it was determined that we would be a good match for each other. Our marriage was a great celebration with friends and family and lots of good food in the traditional Indian way.

Shortly after we married, I told Vinutha of all I was learning and experiencing about God and how I felt my life changing. I was not very good at explaining things to her, but she understood that it was affecting my life at a deep level and was very open to all I shared with her. She opened up her journal and read to me things she had written from books she had read, as well as her personal thoughts. It was clear that the prayers of my friends at church regarding a wife who could share my life on a deep level had been answered.

When we returned to Beaverton, I repeated the Foundations of Christian Faith class with Vinutha. The Foundations of Faith class and water baptism were major steps in solidifying my faith in Christ. It took about three years to begin to fully understand God's love for me and know in my heart that it was not what I did for God that brought me to Him, but what Jesus had done for me.

In 1995, Vinutha became pregnant. At 4½ months we found out that she was carrying twins. We returned to India for family support just in time for her to have the babies. We remained in India for about two years, and I was praying that God would open the door for me to speak to my family about my faith in Christ and the wonderful changes it had brought to my life. They knew we were attending a small church and they respected the positive changes they saw in me, but nobody was responding. I was still the baby of the family. I kept on praying for them.

In 1997, I had the opportunity to take a job in California and we made the move. A year later, I had another opportunity which took me to work for Microsoft in Washington State.

In 2000, I got a call from my brother about my mother's condition. She had been in poor health for 15 years due to diabetes and my father was taking care of her. My brother said she was in a coma and if I wanted to see her, I should come soon. I was really crying out to the Lord. I prayed, "Lord, Your scripture says that if we believe in the Lord Jesus Christ, our whole household will be saved. I believe You are the same yesterday, today and forever. You can raise the dead. You can give sight to the blind. You can heal the sick. Please, heal my mother."

I called my friends, Roy and Arlene, who had treated me like a son at Christ Community Church. I asked them and the church to pray for my mother. My friends at the local church in India were also praying. I told my sisters, "Even though she's not responding, keep talking to her. Tell her that Sri is coming from the U.S."

As soon as the plane landed, I went to the hospital. When I saw her I called out to the Lord in praise. God had really touched her. She had come out of the coma; she was eating, responding and using little words. Soon I was taking her around in the wheelchair, and in 19 days

Hope After Despair

she was normal. I carried her home in my arms.

That was a big miracle. That was a turning point for my family. With their own eyes, they had seen a miracle of God. Everybody had given up hope. People had come from my church there to pray for her, people in the U.S. were praying, and within 19 days, she was home.

My family saw that there was a God that could change lives and heal people, and that was something new for them, just as it had been for me several years before. They had not experienced the things I had been telling them until now. Two of my friends from the local church started visiting my family. They shared the gospel and my family responded very well. My mother was also responding very well. She received Jesus into her heart. My whole family could see the power of God and were listening to the gospel. This was a joyful time for all of us.

Eleven months later, my sister called me in the U.S. to tell me that, again, my mother was very ill and she was dying. I started calling my mother and praying for her. She was mildly responding. While I was praying with her by telephone, my sisters arrived at her home and they told me that her spirit was going away. My mother was passing. After a half hour, I felt God telling me, "She's with me." That gave me a great sense of peace and I knew that this was not a time for mourning, but a time for rejoicing. I felt the Lord saying, "Go, and tell your family members."

When we went home I shared this testimony with my family. Around 250 people were at my mother's funeral. I shared about my mother's faith and what happened in her life, and what hope she had. This is not the usual way with people of my culture when death is near. They are afraid and cry and cry. But my family's experience was something far different with the passing of my mother because of the hope that God gives us. Most of the people at my mother's funeral received the peace of God when they heard of her peaceful passing.

About this time my father also received the Lord and other family members and friends became believers in Jesus as well. The result was the establishment of a small church of about 50 people. Due to persecution in that area of India, it has not been easy for that fledgling group of believers, but miraculously, God takes care of His children.

My life continues in this country with a good job at Microsoft in Washington State. We stay in contact with our friends at Christ Community Church and still feel a part of that fellowship. My wife, Vinutha, is finishing her medical residency to become qualified to practice medicine in the United States. Our twin boys, Adarsh and Anand, are growing well in the Lord by the grace of God. We are still increasing in our faith and thank God for His faithfulness, protection and many blessings in our lives.

Afterword

Maybe you strongly relate to one of the stories you just read. You, or someone close to you, is going through a similar crisis and there seems to be no answer. The purpose of this book is to give you hope because even a tiny glimmer of light, penetrating the darkness, is enough to turn you from despair.

If you will press on just a little further you will find the answer, which these people found. That answer is a person who is very close to you. His name is Jesus and He is listening to your heart. He knows the anguish and discouragement you are feeling. Your journey to hope has already begun. Jesus said, "I came to find and restore the lost."

We are not talking about religion. This is about getting connected with God just by trusting in Him—believing that He cares about you. The Bible says:

"It's the word of faith that welcomes God to go to work and set things right for us..." Say the welcoming word to God—"Jesus is my Master"—embracing, body and soul, God's work of doing in us what He did in raising Jesus from the dead. That's it. You're not "doing" anything; you're simply calling out to God, trusting Him to do it for you. That's salvation. With

Reasons for Hope

your whole being you embrace God setting things right, and then you say it, right out loud: "God has set everything right between Him and me!"

Scripture reassures us, "No one who trusts God like this—heart and soul—will ever regret it." It's exactly the same no matter what a person's religious background may be: the same God for all of us, acting the same incredibly generous way to everyone who calls out for help. "Everyone who calls, 'Help, God!' gets help."
(Romans 10, The Message)

So that's just how close God is to you. Embrace hope by trusting God's loving message to you. Tell Him you need His love and help. He hears and He answers. Then get back to the friend who gave you this book. Tell them what has happened to you. A new adventure has begun. You are a friend of God and the future is filled with hope and a truly good life.

—Pastor Gary Morse

Welcome to the Community!

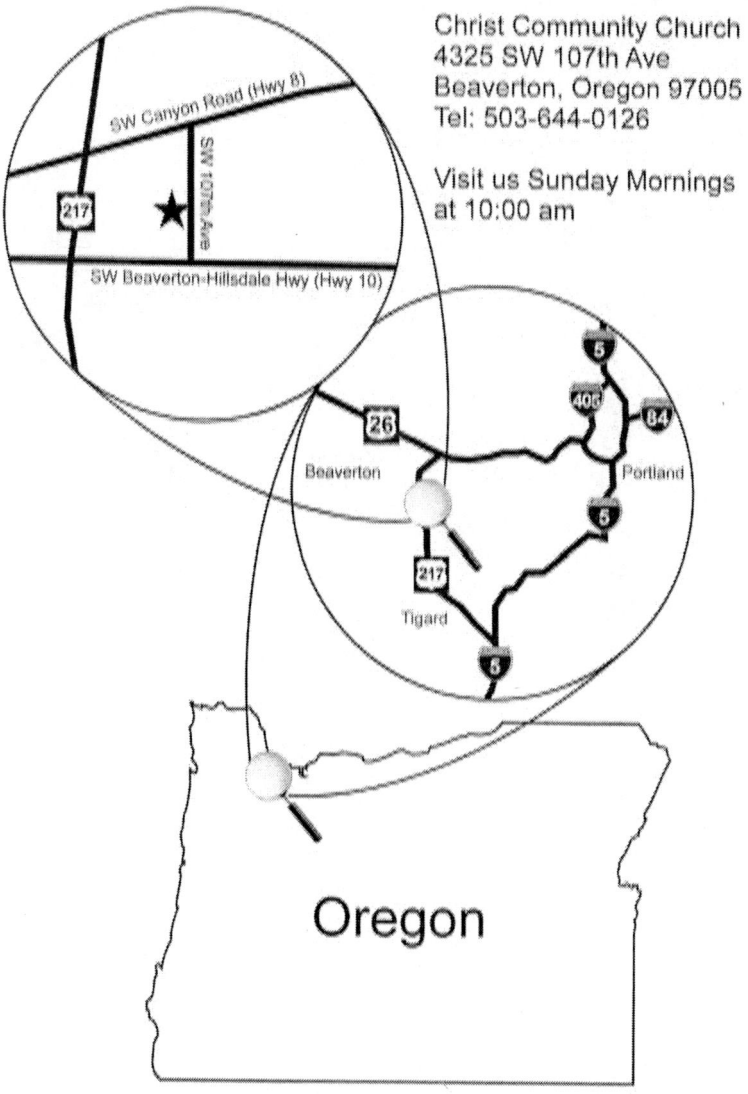

Christ Community Church
4325 SW 107th Ave
Beaverton, Oregon 97005
Tel: 503-644-0126

Visit us Sunday Mornings at 10:00 am

SW Canyon Road (Hwy 8)
SW 107th Ave
217
SW Beaverton-Hillsdale Hwy (Hwy 10)

26
Beaverton
405
5
84
Portland
217
Tigard
5

Oregon

http://www.ReasonsForHope.info

Good Catch Publishing

www.goodcatchpublishing.com